The AICPA
AUDIT COMMITTEE
TOOLKIT

Private Companies, 2nd Edition

15940PRIV-344

In cooperation with: and
Audit Committee Effectiveness Center

Copyright © 2014 by

American Institute of Certified Public Accountants, Inc.

New York, NY 10036-8775

All rights reserved. For information about the procedure for requesting permission to make copies of any part of this work, please email copyright@aicpa.org with your request. Otherwise, requests should be written and mailed to the Permissions Department, AICPA, 220 Leigh Farm Road, Durham, NC 27707-8110.

1 2 3 4 5 6 7 8 9 0 SP 1 9 8 7 6 5 4

ISBN: 978-1-94023-546-2

Publisher: Linda Prentice Cohen
Acquisitions Editor: Robert Fox
Developmental Editor: Suzanne Morgen
Project Manager: Charlotte Ingles

Acknowledgements

The AICPA *Audit Committee Toolkit: Private Companies* was developed by AICPA members working in and with private companies. We are grateful to the members of the task force and the organizations that provided them the opportunity to participate in this project for their dedication, professional expertise, and hard work.

We are pleased to recognize the efforts of the following leaders on the task force:

Audrey Katcher, CPA, CISA, CITP	Chair
Audrey Foster, CPA, CGMA, CITP, CISA	Co-Chair
Bill Johnson, CPA	Co-Chair

Finally, we offer our sincere thanks to Lori A. Sexton, CPA, CGMA, AICPA Technical Manager, and staff liaison, for her oversight and organization of this project. Also recognized is CNA for its continued sponsorship and for making this toolkit and the Audit Committee Effectiveness Center Web site available in support of our members, the organizations that they serve, and the public interest.

Public Company Audit Committee Toolkit Task Force

Stephen G. Austin, CPA, MBA
Swenson Advisors, LLP
San Diego, CA

Audrey Foster, CPA, CGMA, CITP, CISA
AICPA
Durham, NC

Nancy Frazee, CIA, CRMA, CCSA, CIPP
Director of Internal Audit
Kansas City, MO

Bill Johnson, CPA
Vice President and Chief Audit Executive
St. Louis, MO

Audrey Katcher, CPA, CISA, CITP, Partner
RubinBrown LLP
St. Louis, MO

Gail R. Presswood, CPA
Director of Internal Audit
Washington University in St. Louis
St. Louis, MO

Zachary Shelton, CPA
Swenson Advisors, LLP
Murrieta, CA

Jeffrey Sparks, CPA, Partner
RubinBrown, LLP
St. Louis, MO

Preface

Since it was launched in late 2003, the AICPA Audit Committee Effectiveness Center (www. aicpa.org/FORTHEPUBLIC/AUDITCOMMITTEEEFFECTIVENESS/Pages/ACEC.aspx) has earned a reputation as a respected source for audit tools, forms, and information by both AICPA membership and the business public. The Center's two main features—The Audit Committee Toolkit series and the Audit Committee Matching System—are part of the AICPA's continuing efforts to support public interest in audit-related issues.

This 2nd edition of the *Audit Committee Toolkit: Private Companies* is focused solely on public companies, and is designed for use by the following groups:

- All private companies, regardless of size
- Board and audit committee members of private companies
- CEO, CFO, chief audit executives, and other key staff positions of private companies
- External and internal auditors

This edition features updates and revisions that reflect significant changes and updates to the COSO Framework, changes to SEC and *Public Company Accounting Oversight Board* (PCAOB) regulations and standards that have occurred since the last edition, as well as an International Financial Reporting Standards (IFRS) implementation tool.

This toolkit has been organized into the following subgroups:

- Audit Committee Administration
- Audit Committee Key Responsibilities
- Audit Committee Performance Evaluations
- Audit Committee Other Tools (risk management, SEC, resources, IFRS)

This edition of the *Audit Committee Toolkit: Private Companies* is accompanied by a download containing Microsoft Word files of all the tools so you can modify and customize them to fit your audit committee's needs. Visit www.cpa2biz.com/privatecompany to access the files.

The Audit Committee Matching System (ACMS) offers a way to find CPAs who are willing to serve on corporate boards and audit committees. This free service is available to any organization that needs the CPA skillset in those roles. We encourage AICPA members to register on ACMS, and anyone can visit the online Center to search the database based on certain criteria. The AICPA offers no screening of candidates or companies—each party must perform its own due diligence on the other party.

The AICPA is grateful to CNA for its continued sponsorship of the Audit Committee Effectiveness Center. It is through their support that we are able to publish this book.

If you have questions on how to use the tools contained in this book, suggestions for new or additional tools, or other feedback, please write to us at acms@aicpa.org.

Contents

PART I: Audit Committee Administration

Chapter 1
Benefits of a Private Company Audit Committee

> **Overview:** A rapidly evolving regulatory environment and rising expectations of stakeholders have caused many entities to reassess their internal control and risk management practices. While public companies have been most directly and visibly affected by this trend, other organizations—including governmental bodies, not-for-profits, and private companies—have also experienced the impact of the changing compliance culture.
>
> One key area of focus for many organizations has been the establishment and strengthening of audit committees. A well-structured audit committee can be a significant factor in improving overall organizational governance. At the same time, different organizations have different needs and issues, so "one size fits all" approaches are seldom appropriate. While some parts of this chapter might not apply to specific companies due to size, the intention is to provide guidance for both large and small audit committees.
>
> The purpose of this chapter is to discuss the reasons why a private company might consider establishing an audit committee. It is to be used by management and directors in assessing their business objectives and determining whether an audit committee might be right for their organization. However, this is not intended to be all-inclusive guidance, rather a best practice when forming and evaluating a private company audit committee.

The creation of an effective audit committee is one key way of enhancing organizational governance and oversight, and it can help reinforce the company's commitment to developing the proper "tone at the top." However, while audit committees are mandatory for public companies, they are optional for private companies. Likewise, the composition and charter of private company audit committees is subject to much more discretion than is the case for public companies. Thus, as a private company evaluates its governance practices, it is useful to consider the various ways in which an audit committee can be beneficial to the objectives of the organization. Many of these potential benefits are discussed in the following sections.

Financial Benefits

A well-designed and properly functioning system of governance can play a key role in achieving the financial goals of the organization. While an audit committee may not have a significant direct impact on the revenues and expenses of the organization, it can nonetheless foster a culture of compliance and control that will create important collateral financial benefits for the organization. Such benefits can include the following:

- Better financial results:
    - Effective governance practices lead to a more effective internal control system that, when overseen by an audit committee, can help ensure more accurate financial information and reduce the likelihood of fraud.

—An audit committee provides an independent channel for raising and resolving key ethics, compliance, and financial reporting issues, thus helping to prevent or deter violation of corporate policies by employees or management.

—Sound governance practices can reduce the risks of the organization, resulting in lower insurance, legal, and borrowing costs.

—Prudent corporate governance can help create conditions that make the organization a more desirable business partner, leading to expanded opportunities for the business.

- Improved access to capital:

—Just as investors and lenders have come to expect vigorous corporate governance practices in public companies, they are also beginning to have similar expectations for private companies.

—Strong corporate governance enhances the intrinsic value of the entity by lowering the risks for potential acquirers and investors.

—Governance and internal control practices similar to those required of public companies can make it easier for private companies to consider seeking capital in public markets.

Better Decision Making

The establishment of an audit committee can contribute to better management decision making in a number of ways, as follows:

- Ensuring the accuracy of financial reports upon which decisions are based:

—Through a focus on key risks and controls, an audit committee can help to ensure the accuracy, timeliness, and completeness of financial information necessary to manage the business.

—An audit committee can also help to bring added clarity to the roles and responsibilities of the organization's employees, thereby increasing the likelihood that transactions will be properly executed and recorded.

- Enhancing the quality of decision-making processes:

—An audit committee can bring a broader perspective to risk assessment and regulatory compliance matters.

—An audit committee can help to ensure open communication between the board, management of the organization, and external and internal auditors.

—By asking tough questions of top management, audit committee members can add rigor to the process of reaching key decisions.

Stronger Relationships With Stakeholders

Private companies have many key stakeholders, including employees, customers, vendors, investors, lenders, regulators, and community members. Relationships with each of these constituents—both internal and external—can be enhanced by the presence of a properly functioning audit committee. This can occur in the following ways:

- Internal stakeholders:
  - —An effective audit committee can help to set an appropriate "tone at the top" by promoting a culture of integrity and loyalty.
  - — An audit committee represents the interests of all owners of the business, including not only the active owners but also minority owners, less involved family members, and the like.
- External stakeholders:
  - —Strong corporate governance is consistent with a general societal trend toward enhanced independent oversight of business organizations.
  - —An audit committee can instill confidence in business partners, potential investors, and others. It can also add further credibility to contractual relationships with vendors and customers.
  - —Strong governance can lead to increased credibility with IRS, FDA, FTC, and other regulators.

Other Benefits

In addition to the points discussed above, an audit committee can provide other benefits to a private company. These include the following:

- In situations in which private companies anticipate transitions in leadership—for example, in the case of a family-owned business—an audit committee can provide an important channel between the auditors, the current owners and managers, and passive owners. Similarly, an audit committee can help mitigate organizational conflict and provide continuity during the leadership transition.
- In situations in which private companies contemplate entering the public capital markets, a preexisting audit committee can help to facilitate the process and ease the transition to the requirements of Sarbanes-Oxley.

Chapter 2
Audit Committee Member Roles and Responsibilities

Overview: Audit committee roles and responsibilities depend on the board and management structure of a private entity and may not fit all types of arrangements. The content presented in this chapter is a best practice.

Boards of directors are faced with ongoing challenges related to the governance of their organizations, risks associated with achieving their organizations' objectives, and compliance with revised and emerging laws and regulations. Responsibilities are ultimately identified by the Board and assigned to various Board Committees, including the audit committee. Delegation of responsibilities and roles to the audit committee varies from entity to entity and continues to evolve. Beyond their responsibility for ensuring accurate and transparent information to investors and other interested parties, audit committee members are being asked to address increasing challenges.

Audit committees generally consist of a minimum of three independent directors, at least one of whom is a "financial expert." Other key qualifications may include risk management expertise, and broad business or leadership experience. Responsibilities of the audit committee vary from organization to organization.

The following information provides areas to consider as the audit committee's responsibilities are defined, assigned, and implemented. In addition to the items discussed, your entity should consult concurrently with your identified experts, such as legal, accounting, auditing, or compliance.

The audit committee assists the board in its oversight of

- integrity of the company's financial statements;
- internal controls including internal control over financial reporting;
- independent auditor's qualifications, independence, and performance;
- internal audit function's qualifications, independence, and performance;
- the company's risk management and overall governance process; and
- the company's ethics and compliance program, which includes legal and regulatory requirements.

Specific responsibilities assigned to an audit committee are set forth in an audit committee charter that is approved by the board of directors. An audit committee charter should address processes, procedures, and responsibilities. Audit committee responsibilities can vary by company due to factors such as the size of the company (for example, small-cap, mid-cap, or large-cap); type of private company (that is, family-owned, closely held, private companies with registered debt securities; private companies with large outside shareholder bases or an employee stock ownership plan as a shareholder; or private companies having to deal with venture capital investors, lenders, insurers, and pre-initial public offering, among others); stage of development; complexity of the business (for example, a single service or product line, multiple service or product lines, or a global business); and the type of business in which the company is involved (for example, insurance, financial services, manufacturing, telecommunications, retail, or pharmaceutical).

The following illustrative list of responsibilities, which is not intended to be complete, includes both required and best practice for audit committee members.

Audit Committee Process and Procedures

- Develop an audit committee charter and obtain approval from the board of directors.
- Conduct annual review of the audit committee charter.
- Set agenda for the audit committee meetings based upon the audit committee charter and other relevant issues.
- Ensure meeting minutes are prepared.
- Provide audit committee reporting responsibilities to the board of directors.
- Educate the other Board members on the understanding of the financial statements, financial statements risks, and internal controls over financial reporting.
- Prepare annual audit committee report for inclusion in the proxy statement.
- Conduct annual self-assessment of effectiveness and efficiency of the audit committee.
- Conduct regularly scheduled and documented meetings with the independent external auditor, chief audit executive (leader of the internal audit function), as well as the general counsel, CEO, CFO, senior business leaders, and others as needed. These meetings are generally conducted in executive session at the conclusion of each regularly scheduled meeting.
- Consider development of an annual calendar based upon audit committee charter.

Oversight of the Financial Reporting Process

- Review critical accounting policies, practices, judgments, estimates, significant issues, significant transactions, adjustments, unusual items, complex issues, and business arrangements.
- Review annual and interim financial statements and management's discussion and analysis.
- Review earnings releases and information provided to analysts and rating agencies.
- Obtain explanations from management on all significant variances.
- Question management and the independent auditor on significant financial reporting issues.

- Review comparative data from other companies within the industry to perform reasonableness tests of the company's results.

- Facilitate the resolution of disagreements between management and the independent auditor regarding financial reporting issues.

- Determine when a subject matter expert is required and hire advisers when needed.

- Review management letters containing the recommendations of the independent auditor and management's responses to those recommendations.

- Determine that adequate procedures are in place for the review of the company's disclosure of financial information extracted or derived from the company's financial statements and assess periodically the adequacy of these procedures.

- Understand complex accounting and reporting areas and how management addresses them.

- Understand significant judgments and estimates used by management and their impact on the financial statements, such as fair-value accounting and related assumptions.

- Review new accounting and reporting requirements, and assess how pending financial reporting and regulatory developments may affect the company.

- Discuss succession planning for the CFO and staff. Understand management incentives, perhaps through periodic discussions with the compensation committee, and assess their impact on the financial reporting process. Consider whether the incentive structure contributes to an increased fraud risk.

Oversight of Financial Reporting

- Oversee adequacy of the company's system of internal controls and consider compliance with Sarbanes Oxley section 404 attestations (that is, if in pre-public offering phase).

- Determine if the company has adopted an internal control framework, such as COSO in the establishment of their system of internal controls.

- Review development and implementation of a sub-certification process over internal controls and compliance with related Sarbanes Oxley section 404 attestations.

Oversight of the Independent Auditor

- Review audit plan and scope of audit to be conducted by the independent auditor.

- Provide pre-approval of all audits, permitted non-audit services, and proposed fees.

- Appoint or replace the independent auditor, including the periodic rotation of the audit partner.

- Conduct evaluations of the independent auditor. Meet periodically with tax, IT, SEC, and other specialists.

Oversight of the Internal Audit Function

- Approve the internal audit department charter.

- Ensure that the internal audit department follows the Institute of Internal Auditors International Standards for the Professional Practice of Internal Auditing, and maintains an effective quality assessment and improvement program.

- Concur in the appointment of the chief audit executive.
- Review the internal audit department's planning and risk assessment process.
- Review and approve the internal audit department's annual (or periodic) audit plan and scope of audits to be conducted.
- Conduct evaluations of chief audit executive.
- Ensure that the chief audit executive reports functionally to the audit committee and administratively to senior management.

Oversight of Risk Management

- Oversee system of risk assessment and risk management as determined by the board of directors. The audit committee should be focused primarily on financial risk.
- Oversee and respond to enterprise risk management activities.
- Periodically reassess the list of top enterprise risks, determining who in the management committee is responsible for each risk.

Oversight of Ethics and Compliance

- Oversee system for compliance with legal and regulatory requirements.
- Ensure that management exhibits ethical behavior and reported violations receive action.
- Ensure that a code of conduct has been developed, reviewed, and updated as needed, and that all employees are given the code of conduct, understand it, and receive training on a regular basis.
- Ensure that a chief ethics and compliance officer or equivalent has been appointed and has sufficient personnel and resources commensurate with company needs.
- Review the company's procedures for reporting problems, including whistleblower hotline and other communication methods.
- Establish a process for audit committee special investigations, including but not limited to whistleblower allegation, anti-fraud plan compliance, discovery of error, and illegal acts.
- Ensure that the chief ethics and compliance officer or equivalent has direct access to the board or one of its committees.

Limitation of Audit Committee's Role

While the audit committee has the responsibilities set forth in its charter, it is not the responsibility of the audit committee to plan or conduct routine audits or to be the primary determinant that the company's financial statements and disclosures are complete and accurate and are in accordance with generally accepted accounting principles and applicable rules and regulations. These tasks are the responsibility of management and the independent auditor, and the audit committee has an oversight responsibility to see that the objective is achieved.

Chapter 3
Audit Committee Charter Matrix

Overview: Preparing an audit committee charter is a best practice for private companies because it creates a clear awareness of the committee's key responsibilities. However, the charter is often prepared and forgotten except for its annual review. This matrix is designed to help audit committees make the charter a living document and use it to manage the agenda. This tool is meant as a sample. Users of the tool should put their own charters in the first column and use this example as a guide for defining the steps to accomplish each objective, the associated performance measure, and the scheduling. The audit committee charter presented in the first column of the following matrix is just an example of a best practice charter. It includes the requirements of the Sarbanes-Oxley Act of 2002 (the Act) and stock exchange requirements, which are not requirements in a private company charter, but may want to be considered as a best practice.

Audit Committee Charter Matrix for the Year Ending: _____

Audit Committee Charter	Steps to Accomplish the Objective	Deliverable	When to Achieve (Frequency Due Date)	Date Completed
1. Each member of the audit committee shall be a member of the board of directors, in good standing, and shall be independent in order to serve on this committee.	Test for independence, based on the regulations under the Act and any other regulations that may be operative. Although a best practice, the independence requirement of the Act does not apply to private companies.	Indicate in the audit committee minutes whenever a new member is appointed; acknowledge that independence has been verified.	Affirm annually or whenever a change in status by any audit committee member occurs.	
2. At least one member of the audit committee shall be designated as a *financial expert*. (See chapter 4, "Audit Committee Financial Expert Decision Tree," in this toolkit.)	Ascertain that at least one member of the audit committee meets the requirements of a financial expert under the regulations of the Act. Although a best practice, the independence requirement of the Act does not apply to private companies.	Indicate in audit committee meeting minutes which member of the audit committee is designated as the financial expert.	Affirm annually, unless there is a change in status.	
3. Review the audit committee's charter annually, reassess the adequacy of this charter, and recommend any proposed changes to the board of directors. Consider changes that are necessary as a result of new laws or regulations.	Review the charter each year. Assess the appropriateness of each point in the charter in light of the previous year's experience. Assess the completeness of the charter in light of new best practices and new legal or regulatory requirements.	Report to the board on the appropriateness of the audit committee charter and any revisions recommended.	Review annually, unless changes are needed during the course of the year.	

Audit Committee Charter	Steps to Accomplish the Objective	Deliverable	When to Achieve (Frequency Due Date)	Date Completed
4. The audit committee shall meet at least four times per year, and each time the company proposes to issue a press release with its quarterly or annual earnings information. These meetings may be combined with regularly scheduled meetings, or more frequently meetings, as circumstances may require. The audit committee may ask members of management or others to attend the meetings and provide pertinent information as necessary.	In-person meetings should be held at least once each quarter. All members are expected to attend each meeting in person, or via telephone conference or videoconference. Telephone conference meetings may be held more frequently. The agendas for meetings should be prepared and provided to members in advance, along with appropriate briefing materials.	Prepare minutes that document decisions made and action steps following meetings and review for approval. Meeting minutes should be filed with the board of directors.	Minutes should be distributed as soon as possible but no later than prior to the next meeting.	
5. Conduct executive sessions with the independent auditors, chief executive officer (CEO), chief financial officer (CFO), chief audit executive (CAE), and anyone else as desired by the committee.	Establish these sessions in conjunction with quarterly meetings or as necessary. (See chapter 13, "Guidelines and Questions for Conducting an Audit Committee Executive Session," in this toolkit.)	Develop action steps to be taken if appropriate.	Review quarterly and as necessary.	

(continued)

Audit Committee Charter	Steps to Accomplish the Objective	Deliverable	When to Achieve (Frequency Due Date)	Date Completed
6. The audit committee shall be authorized to hire outside counsel or other consultants as necessary. This may take place any time during the year. (See chapter 8, "Engaging Independent Counsel and Other Advisers," in this toolkit.)	Requests for proposals (RFPs) should be used, if time permits.	Report submitted by outside counsel or consultant.	Review as needed.	
7. Review and concur in the appointment, replacement, reassignment, or dismissal of the CAE. (See chapter 7, "Guidelines for Hiring the Chief Audit Executive (CAE)," in this toolkit.)	Meet in executive session at each meeting with the CAE to allow assessment and feedback. Hold special meetings as may be necessary to address appointment, reassignment, or dismissal of CAE. The audit committee chair should be available if any unforeseen issues arise between meetings relating to the CAE. Meet at least once annually with other members of executive management and the independent auditors to discuss the performance of the CAE. Discuss job satisfaction and other employment issues with the CAE.	Report to the full board on the performance of the CAE, including the effectiveness of the internal audit function.	Conduct ongoing reviews, as changes can be made at any time during the year.	

Audit Committee Charter	Steps to Accomplish the Objective	Deliverable	When to Achieve (Frequency Due Date)	Date Completed
8. Appoint the independent auditors to be engaged by the company, establish the audit fees of the independent auditors, pre-approve any non-audit services provided by the independent auditors, including tax services, before the services are rendered. Review and evaluate the performance of the independent auditors and review with the full board of directors any proposed discharge of the independent auditors. (See the tools and guidance in chapter 5, "Sample Request for Proposal Letter for CPA Services (Private Company)," and chapter 6, "AICPA Peer Review and PCAOB Inspections of CPA Firms: An Overview," in this toolkit.)	At least once each year, discuss each of these items with management, the CAE, and the board of directors. Review total audit fee in relation to any non-audit services being provided by the independent auditor. Discuss the audit committee's review of the independent auditors with the board of directors. Ascertain that the independent auditors do not perform any non-audit service that is prohibited by Section 201 of the Act, the PCAOB, or any other regulator or body that has authority in this area. Consider establishing pre-defined acceptable services the independent auditor may engage in based upon regulations. Although a best practice, the limitations on non-audit work performed by the independent auditors in the Act do not apply to private companies.	Report on and recommend the performance and fees paid to the independent auditors. Review the scope of all services provided by the independent audit firm throughout the organization.	Review soon after year-end, so that the recommendation for the appointment of the independent auditor can be included in the proxy statement.	

(continued)

Audit Committee Charter	Steps to Accomplish the Objective	Deliverable	When to Achieve (Frequency Due Date)	Date Completed
9. Ascertain that the lead (or concurring) independent audit partner does not serve in that capacity for more than five of the company's fiscal years. In addition, ascertain that any partner other than the lead or concurring partner does not serve more than seven years at the partner level on the company's audit committee.	Establish when the five-year limit will be reached for the current lead independent audit partner. At least a year prior to that time, discuss transition plans for the new lead independent audit partner. Although a best practice, the partner rotation requirements do not apply to private companies.	Document these discussions in audit committee meeting minutes.	Review annually with the independent auditors.	
10. Review with management the policies and procedures with respect to officers' expense accounts and perquisites, including their use of corporate assets, and consider the results of any review of these areas by the internal auditor or the independent auditors.	Review policies and procedures annually. Discuss with the CAE the need for testing by either the internal auditors, independent auditors, or other parties.	Report issues, if any, to the board.	Review policies and procedures at a regularly scheduled meeting, and discuss audit plan. Review any significant findings as they arise.	

Audit Committee Charter	Steps to Accomplish the Objective	Deliverable	When to Achieve (Frequency Due Date)	Date Completed
11. Consider with management the rationale for employing audit firms and other outside specialists other than the principal independent auditors.	Establish a policy for the audit committee to pre-approve engaging auditors other than the principal independent auditors. Use RFPs for engaging auditors or other professionals for non-audit or other services that the independent auditor cannot perform. Review compliance with the policy by management. (See chapter 5, "Sample Request for Proposal Letter for CPA Services and Qualifications (Private Company)," in this toolkit.)	Document auditor selection criteria. Also, use a decision matrix to evaluate and document the third party selection. Prepare an engagement letter for each engagement.	Continually review the policy and the company's compliance with it. Other auditors may need to be hired at any point during the year.	
12. Make inquiries to management, the CAE, and the independent auditors about significant risks or exposures facing the company; assess the steps management has taken or proposes to take to minimize such risks to the company; and periodically review compliance with such steps.	Create a portfolio that documents the material risks that the company faces. Update as events occur. Review with management and the CAE quarterly or sooner if necessary, to make sure it is up to date.	Submit a risk report including mitigation strategies, quantifiable risks, and insurance to cover such risks as loss of business.	Review at least once each year, and more frequently if necessary.	

(continued)

Audit Committee Charter	Steps to Accomplish the Objective	Deliverable	When to Achieve (Frequency Due Date)	Date Completed
(See the tools and guidance included in chapter 9, "Internal Control: Guidelines and Tool for the Audit Committee," chapter 10, "Fraud and the Responsibilities of the Audit Committee: An Overview," and chapter 20, "Enterprise Risk Management: A Tool for Strategic Oversight," in this toolkit.)				
13. Review the audit scope and plan of the internal auditors and the independent auditors with the independent auditor, the controller of the company, and the CAE. Address the coordination of audit efforts to assure the completeness of coverage, reduction of redundant efforts, and the effective use of audit resources.	Meet with the independent audit partner, the controller, and CAE to discuss the scope of the previous year's audit and lessons learned. Later, discuss planned scope for audit of current year.	Document the meeting in the audit committee meeting minutes.	At the second quarter meeting each year, review the scope of the previous year's audit, and the inter-relationship between the internal and independent auditors with respect to the scope of the independent auditors' work.	

Audit Committee Charter	Steps to Accomplish the Objective	Deliverable	When to Achieve (Frequency Due Date)	Date Completed
14. Review with management and the CAE: • significant findings on internal audits during the year, and management's responses thereto. • any difficulties the internal audit team encountered in the course of their audits, including any restrictions on the scope of their work or access to required information. • any changes required in the scope of their internal audit. • the internal auditing department budget and staffing.	Review and discuss the findings for each audit completed since the prior meeting, and management's response to the report. Discuss internal audit department budget and staffing with CAE. Discuss internal audit's compliance with the Institute of Internal Auditors' (IIA) standards, including the requirement for a peer review once every five years.		No later than the third quarter meeting each year, review the plans for the audit of the current year.	

(continued)

Audit Committee Charter	Steps to Accomplish the Objective	Deliverable	When to Achieve (Frequency Due Date)	Date Completed
• the internal auditing department charter. • internal auditing's compliance with IIA's Standards for the Professional Practice of Internal Auditing (standards).				
15. Inquire of the CEO, CFO, controller, independent auditor, and anyone else desired by the audit committee, regarding the quality of earnings of the company from a subjective as well as an objective standpoint.	Discuss quality of earnings with the CEO, CFO, controller, independent auditor, and other executives. Identify any issues addressed, and their resolution.	Include in agenda for executive sessions. (See chapter 13, "Guidelines and Questions for Conducting an Audit Committee Executive Session," in this toolkit.)	Review, as necessary, but at least annually.	
16. Review with the independent accountants and the CAE • the adequacy of the company's internal controls including computerized information system controls and security.	Review key internal controls with the CAE, and understand how these controls will be tested during the year.	Report to the board of directors on issues relating to internal controls, with emphasis on management's ability to override and related monitoring and testing.	Submit a comprehensive report to the board at the second quarter meeting each year.	

Audit Committee Charter	Steps to Accomplish the Objective	Deliverable	When to Achieve (Frequency Due Date)	Date Completed
• any related significant findings and recommendations of the independent auditors and internal audit services together with management's responses thereto. (See the tools and guidance included in chapter 9, "Internal Control: Guidelines and Tool for the Audit Committee," chapter 10, "Fraud and the Responsibilities of the Audit Committee: An Overview," and chapter 15, "Responding to the Identification of a Material Weakness in Internal Control: A Checklist for the Audit Committee," in this toolkit.)	Review these plans with the independent auditor to understand their scope with respect to key controls. Review with the CAE the plans for audits of other elements of the control environment. Determine that all internal control weaknesses are quantified, reviewed, and addressed.		Update on anything new, or any changes to the internal control system, at every meeting.	

(continued)

Audit Committee Charter	Steps to Accomplish the Objective	Deliverable	When to Achieve (Frequency Due Date)	Date Completed
17. Review with management and the independent auditor the effect of any new regulatory and accounting initiatives.	Independently, through professional reading and CPE, keep up to date on new developments related to the industry, and the environment in which the company operates, including any regulatory requirements to which it may be subject. Discuss with management and the independent auditors in meetings.	Record discussion and any action steps in audit committee meeting minutes.	Review as necessary.	
18. Review with each public accounting firm that performs an audit: • All critical accounting policies and practices used by the company. • All alternative treatments of financial information within generally accepted accounting principles that have been discussed with management of the company, the ramifications of each alternative, and the treatment preferred by the company. (See the tool in chapter 12, "Issues Report from Management," in this toolkit.)	Discuss each matter and related matters that may come to the attention of the audit committee or the independent auditors through this process. Create an action plan and follow-up plan as necessary.	Submit reports and documentation of discussions and resolution of disagreements.	Review, at least annually, and in conjunction with the year-end audit.	

Audit Committee Charter	Steps to Accomplish the Objective	Deliverable	When to Achieve (Frequency Due Date)	Date Completed
19. Review all material written communications between the independent auditors and management, such as any management letter or schedule of unadjusted differences.	Discuss each item with the independent auditors and management, including the CAE, and conclude on the appropriateness of the proposed resolution.	Submit reports and documentation of discussions, resolution of issues, and the action plan for any items requiring follow up and monitoring.	Review at the completion of the independent audit.	
20. Review with management and the independent auditors • the company's annual financial statements and related footnotes. • the independent auditors' audit of the financial statements and their report thereon. • the independent auditors' judgments about the quality, not just the acceptability, of the company's accounting principles as applied in its financial reporting.	Discuss each matter, and others that may come to the attention of the audit committee through this process, with management (including the CAE) and the independent auditors. Review with management the course of action to be taken for any action requiring follow up. Monitor any follow-up action that requires continued audit committee intervention. (See the tool in chapter 14, "Independent Auditor Communications with Audit Committee," in this toolkit.)	Submit reports and documentation of discussions, resolution of disagreements, or action plan for any item requiring follow up.	Review at the completion of the independent audit.	

(continued)

Audit Committee Charter	Steps to Accomplish the Objective	Deliverable	When to Achieve (Frequency Due Date)	Date Completed
• any significant changes required in the independent auditors' audit plan. • any serious difficulties or disputes with management encountered during the audit. • matters required to be discussed by Statement on Auditing Standards (SAS) No. 114, *The Auditor's Communication With Those Charged with Governance* (AICPA, *Professional Standards*, AU sec. 380), as amended, related to the conduct of the audit.				
21. Review with the general counsel and the CAE legal and regulatory matters that, in the opinion of management, may have a material impact on the financial statements, related company compliance policies, and programs and reports received from regulators.	Discuss whether the company is in compliance with laws and regulations that govern the environment(s) and industry(ies) in which it operates, as well as other applicable laws and regulations.	Report to the board that the review has taken place and any matters that need to be brought to its attention.	Review at each meeting.	

Audit Committee Charter	Steps to Accomplish the Objective	Deliverable	When to Achieve (Frequency Due Date)	Date Completed
22. Periodically review the company's code of conduct to ensure that it is adequate and up to date. Review with the CAE and the company's general counsel the results of their review of the monitoring of compliance with the company's code of conduct.	Review results with the CAE and general counsel. Consider any adjustments that may be necessary to the company's code of conduct. Consider steps that may need to be taken to ensure that compliance is at the highest possible level.	Report to the board that the review of the code of conduct was done. Recommend changes to the code of conduct to the board as needed.	Review annually at the fourth-quarter meeting. Review any significant findings as they arise.	
23. Review the policy and procedures for the receipt, retention, and treatment of complaints received by the company regarding illegal or unethical behavior, violations of law, regulation, rule or policy of the company, accounting, internal accounting controls, or auditing matters that may be submitted by any party internal or external to the organization. Review any such complaints that might have been received, current status, and resolution, if one has been reached.	Review procedures with the CAE and the general counsel. Review all complaints that have been received and the status of resolution. Ensure that proper steps are taken to investigate complaints and resolve timely. (See also the tool in chapter 11, "Whistleblower Policy: Complaint Reporting Procedures and Tracking," in this toolkit.)	Review an original of each complaint received, no matter the media used to submit. Discuss the status or resolution of each complaint. Review a cumulative list of complaints submitted to date to review for patterns or other observations.	Review at each meeting.	

(continued)

Audit Committee Charter	Steps to Accomplish the Objective	Deliverable	When to Achieve (Frequency Due Date)	Date Completed
24. The audit committee will perform other functions as assigned by law, the company's charter or bylaws, or the board of directors.	Monitor developments in the regulatory, legislative, and legal environments, and respond to any new requirements as needed.		Review new business at all meetings.	
25. The audit committee will evaluate the independent auditors and internal auditors.	Use information from executive sessions conducted throughout the year. Use a formal assessment tool for each group. (See the tools and guidance in chapter 16, "Evaluating the Internal Audit Function: Questions to Consider," and chapter 17, "Evaluating the Independent Auditor: Questions to Consider" in this toolkit.)	Submit recommendations for changes in process and procedures. For independent auditors, request RFPs, if changes are being considered.	Review after completion of the annual audit.	
26. The audit committee will review its effectiveness.	The audit committee will conduct a self-assessment and 360-degree evaluation of all members. (See the tools and guidance in chapter 18, "Conducting an Audit Committee Self-Evaluation: Questions to Consider," in this toolkit.)	Discuss recommendations for improving the effectiveness of the audit committee with the board of directors (BOD). Record in BOD minutes.	Review annually.	

Audit Committee Charter	Steps to Accomplish the Objective	Deliverable	When to Achieve (Frequency Due Date)	Date Completed
27. Create an audit committee calendar for the ensuing year or review and approve the agenda submitted by the CAE.	Complete the "Audit Committee Charter Matrix." (Use this tool as a sample and tailor it to your organization.)		Review at the fourth quarter meeting for the upcoming year.	

Chapter 4
Audit Committee Financial Expert Decision Tree

> **Overview:** While there is no explicit requirement for a private company audit committee to include a member having some level of financial expertise, it is considered a best practice. In addition, it should be the goal of the private company audit committee that all its members have some level of experience in financial matters. The following decision tree illustrates how the audit committee might evaluate a candidate for consideration as a financial expert. See chapter 21, "SEC Final Rule on Audit Committee Financial Experts," for more information on defining the term *financial expert*.

Audit Committee Financial Expertise

The following attributes are all deemed to be typical components of financial expertise:

- An understanding of generally accepted accounting principles, generally accepted auditing standards, and financial statements
- The ability to assess the general application of such principles and standards in connection with the accounting for estimates, accruals, and reserves
- Experience preparing, auditing, analyzing, or evaluating financial statements that present a breadth and level of complexity of accounting issues that can reasonably be expected to be raised by the organization's financial statements or experience actively supervising (that is, direct involvement with) one or more people engaged in such activities
- An understanding of internal controls and procedures for financial reporting
- An understanding of audit committee functions
- A general understanding of the financial issues and specific knowledge of the sector (for example, health care, manufacturing, and financial services, among others) in which the organization participates

The following questions may be used to assess whether an individual audit committee member, or the committee as a whole, possesses the preceding attributes:

- Have one or more individuals completed a program of learning in accounting or auditing?
- Do one or more individuals have experience as a chief or principal financial officer (for example, finance director or business manager), principal accounting officer, controller, public accountant, or auditor?
- Do one or more individuals have experience in position(s) that involve the performance of similar functions?
- Have one or more individuals gained experience by actively supervising a person or people performing one or more of these functions?

- Do one or more individuals have experience overseeing or assessing the performance of companies, or public accountants with respect to the preparation, auditing, or evaluation of financial statements?

- Do one or more individuals have other relevant financial experience (for example, service on boards of banking or investment institutions or experience as a banker or investment adviser)?

- Do one or more individuals have experience serving on audit committees of other companies?

Alternative Approaches

If no individual member of the audit committee possesses the attributes required for financial expertise, and the committee members collectively do not possess such attributes, two options might be considered:

- Engage a financial professional to provide financial expertise as a consultant to the audit committee. Such an individual must otherwise be independent with respect to the organization (that is, must have no other financial arrangements with the organization).

- Pursue a training program for audit committee members to develop the financial expertise. Such training can include participation in professional development programs offered by the AICPA, associations, or the specific sector in which the organization participates, or in-house training programs led by members of the organization's financial management team.

Audit Committee Financial Expert

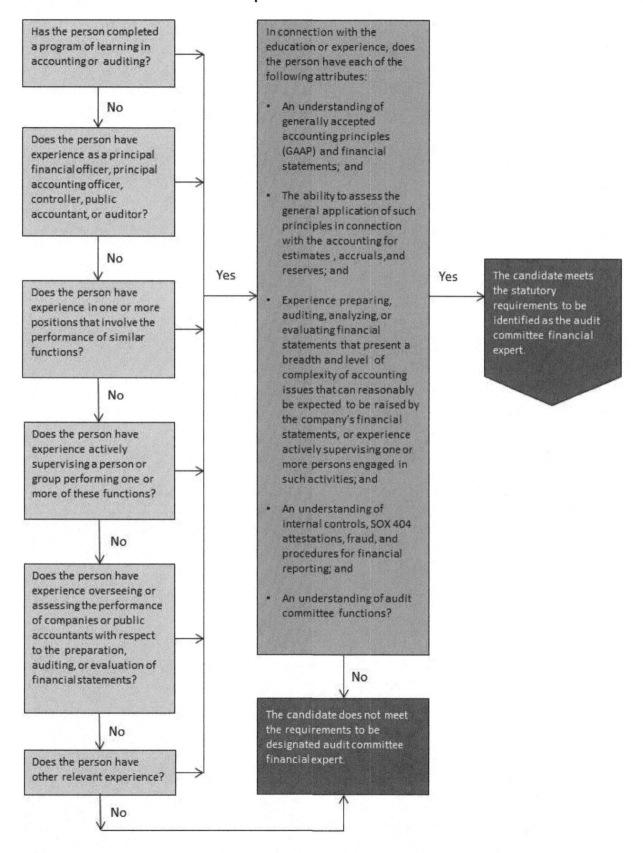

Chapter 5

Sample Request for Proposal Letter for CPA Services and Qualifications (Private Company)

Overview: This tool contains sample language that may be used by a privately held company's management team to request proposal letters from qualified CPA firms when seeking a new service provider. As such, the sample letter may be subject to audit committee review or discussion. Separate requests for proposal (RFPs) could be used for audit services and any additional CPA services (for example, tax or compilations).

Special considerations may be required for private companies operating in regulated industries (for example, banking or insurance), companies planning an initial public offering (IPO), or private equity groups. This sample RFP includes examples of possible verbiage to consider in these situations; however, it does not address all possible issues. Examples of additional information for regulated entities are included in the following sample letter in **bold and italicized type** (for example, special reporting requirements), companies planning an IPO are in <u>double underscored type</u> (for example, due diligence, prospectus, and registration), and information for private equity groups is in *italicized type* (that is, analyzing FASB Interpretation No. 46, *Consolidation of Variable Interest Entities*, identifying tax opportunities to improve cash flow, evaluating equity plan structures, and analyzing private equity pension plans).

Additional useful information in the RFP process is included in chapter 6, "AICPA Peer Reviews of CPA Firms: An Overview," and chapter 17, "Evaluating the Independent Auditor: Questions to Consider" in this toolkit. Consideration of the information included in these sections is critical to successfully evaluating the RFP process.

Because the RFPs may require significant time investments from both the organization, to prepare them, and the CPA firms, to respond fully, the organization may first want to send requests for qualifications to determine the most qualified firms from which to request RFPs.

[*Company Letterhead*]

[*Current Date*]
[*Managing Partner*]
[*CPA Firm*]
[*Street Address*]
[*City, State, Zip*]

Dear Sir or Madam:

Our company is accepting proposals from CPA firms to provide audit and tax services for our company in the future. We invite your firm to submit a proposal to us by _____[Date]_____ for consideration. Note that the audit committee of the company's board of directors (audit committee) is the decision-maker in the hiring of the company's auditor in accordance with the *Sarbanes-Oxley Act of 2002* (the Act). The company is acting at the direction of the Audit Committee in sending this Request for Proposal to you. A description of the company, the services needed, and other pertinent information follow.

Background of ABC Company

ABC Company is a manufacturer of widgets **and is closely regulated by T4M Agency**. Annual revenues are between $40 and $50 million per year, and the company employs 35 people, mostly on the shop floor, and all in one location. The company is family-owned, has a 20-year history of profitability, and is planning an initial public offering (IPO) for January 1, 20XX. [For private equity groups, replace the previous sentence with "The company is a private equity firm and has a XX-year history of profitability or is owned by a private equity firm."] The company has a June 20 fiscal year end, with a requirement to file an audited financial statement with the **bank and certain other regulatory financial reports with the agency** by September 30 of each year.

Services to Be Performed

Your proposal is expected to cover the following services:

1. Annual audit and **regulatory reporting** to be completed in accordance with aforementioned filing requirement(s).

2. Tax filings for the company and its subsidiaries.

3. Compiling of personal tax filings for the top five executives in the company.

4. Assisting in analyzing FASB Interpretation No. 46, *Consolidation of Variable Interest Entities*, and potential impacts on the firm.

5. Evaluating equity plan structures.

6. Analyzing the firm's private equity pension plan for tax deferral opportunities.

7. Providing an IPO advisory engagement,[1] including

---

[1] Note that you may need to determine if there are any independence issues in providing these services.

a. *project management (preparation for the quotation process, assistance in evaluating sponsors, coordination of all required external advisers and underwriters);*

b. *preparation of the business plan;*

c. *strategic review;*

d. *assisting with the SEC registration, including due diligence, the makeup of the registration statement and the federal, state, and National Association of Securities Dealers' approval required for your registration statement to become effective;*

e. *reviewing drafts of the prospectus or offering memorandum (business description; information on the equity, financial position, and economic results; information related to recent results; and future projections); and*

f. *advising on reporting obligations and federal securities laws when the offering is complete, including determining when to bring in an underwriter and legal firm.*

8. Auditor evaluation of and reporting on the internal control over financial reporting.

9. Attendance and reporting to the Audit Committee twice each year.

Key Personnel

Following is a list of key persons you may wish to contact with respect to this engagement:

Mr. Green	CEO	1-123/555-7890
Ms. Brown	CFO	1-123/555-7891
Mr. Black	General Counsel	1-123/555-7892
Mr. White	Controller	1-123/555-7893
Mr. Plain	Chairman	1-123/555-4567
Ms. Trane	Audit Comm. Chair	1-456/555-0123
Mr. Carr	Outside Counsel	1-789/555-9870

For control purposes, we ask that you coordinate requests for additional information, visits to our site, review of prior financial statements and tax returns, and/or appointments with the CEO, CFO, and Audit Committee Chair through our controller, Mr. White.

Relationship With Prior CPA Service Provider

Because the company was founded over 20 years ago, these services have been provided by XYZ CPAs. However, that firm is no longer able to provide the services to our company. In preparing your proposal, be advised that management will give you permission to contact the prior auditors.

> You may use this section to disclose whether the decision to change auditors is a function of changes in your organization, changes in the audit firm, or result of a period review of your satisfaction with the services provided. You may describe other aspects of your relationship with the prior auditor that you are willing to disclose at this stage in the proposal process here. CPA firms may request additional information, which you may choose to disclose only if the CPA firm signs a nondisclosure agreement.

Other Information

Use this space to discuss other information that a CPA firm may need to make an informed proposal on the accounting and/or auditing work that you require. For example, you may need to state that the T4M Agency requires the use of a specific basis of accounting, while the bank requires generally accepted accounting principles. As mentioned earlier, you should only disclose information here that you are comfortable disclosing; additional information may be available to the CPA firms interested in making serious proposals only after signing a nondisclosure agreement.

Your Response to This Request for Proposal

In responding to this request, please provide the following information:

These are sample questions that you may consider asking. You should tailor these questions to your circumstances, and delete or add additional questions as appropriate.

Background on the Firm

1. Detail your firm's experience in providing auditing and tax services to companies in the manufacturing sector, as well as companies of a comparable size to ABC Company.

2. Research whether you provide services to any company(ies) that compete with ABC.

3. Research whether any company(ies) for whom you provide services are part of our value chain—as either a supplier or customer of ABC. Discuss commitments you will make to staff continuity, including your staff turnover experience in the last three years.

4. Identify the five largest clients your firm (or office) has lost in the past three years and the reasons. Also, discuss instances when loss of the client was due to an unresolved auditing or accounting matter. Explain your strategies to resolve the issue(s).

5. Describe how your firm will approach the audit of the organization, including the use of any association or affiliate member firm personnel and the areas that will receive primary emphasis. Also, discuss the firm's use of technology in the audit. Finally, discuss the communication process used by the firm to discuss issues with the management and audit committees of the board.

6. Furnish current standard billing rates for classes of professional personnel for each of the last three years, including an expense policy describing how incidental costs (for example, travel and mileage) are billed.

7. Describe how you bill for questions on technical matters that may arise throughout the year.

8. Provide the names and contact information of other similarly sized clients of the partner and manager that will be assigned to our company.

9. Provide the names and contact information of at least two to three other similarly sized clients of the partner and manager who will be assigned to our company.

10. Describe how and why your firm is different from other firms being considered, and why our selection of your firm as our independent auditors is the best decision we could make.

11. Describe how important ABC Company would be to your firm.

12. Include a copy of your firm's most recent Peer Review report, the related letters of comments, and the firm's response to the letters of comments.

13. Describe the firm's approach to the resolution of technical disagreements (*a*) among engagement personnel, and (*b*) between the firm and the client.

14. Explain whether your firm is independent of ABC and how you arrived at that determination.

15. Explain how you monitor and maintain your independence on an ongoing basis.

Experience in Our Industry

> Use this space to ask questions about the firm's experience providing services to other companies in your industry, as well as providing services to companies within your value chain—either as suppliers or customers.

Expected Approach to This Audit

1. Identify the partner, manager, and in-charge accountant who will be assigned to this audit if you are successful in your bid, and provide biographical material for each. Indicate any complaints against them that have been leveled by the state board of accountancy or other regulatory authority, if any. Indicate any corrective actions that have been taken by the firm with respect to these people.

2. Describe how your firm will approach the audit of the company, including the use of any association or affiliate member firm personnel.

3. Set forth your fee proposal for the 20XX audit with whatever guarantees you offer regarding fee increases in future years. Provide your proposed fee for the quarterly review work that will be required as well as the corporate tax preparation if you are proposing to perform the tax work. Ensure that the fee as proposed is sufficient to cover the work that you expect to perform if you are awarded this audit.

Evaluation of Proposals

The Audit Committee of the Board of Directors of ABC Company will evaluate proposals on a qualitative basis. This includes a review of the firm's peer review and related materials, interviews with senior engagement personnel to be assigned to our company, results of discussions with other clients, and the firm's completeness and timeliness in its response to us. Finally, please submit information on the firm's liability insurance coverage.

If you choose to respond to this request, please do so by [*Date indicated earlier in the letter*].

Sincerely,

Ms. Brown, CPA   Ms. Trane
Chief Financial Officer   Chair
                                           Audit Committee

Chapter 6

AICPA Peer Reviews and PCAOB Inspections of CPA Firms: An Overview

> **Overview:** The tool in this chapter is designed to educate audit committee members about the AICPA practice-monitoring programs (also known as peer review) over the accounting and auditing practices of the majority of U.S. CPA firms. This tool is intended to assist audit committee members in understanding the obligations and oversight of CPA firms. In addition, CPA firms that audit public companies are subject to periodic inspections by the PCAOB. See the section "PCAOB Inspection" of this tool for a discussion of PCAOB inspection and related questions for the audit committee. While this toolkit is focused on private companies, the audit committee can still gain insight from a CPA firm's PCAOB report. It is important to note that the AICPA Peer Review Programs and the PCAOB Inspection Program are not substitutes for each other.

Peer Review of a CPA Firm

This tool will help audit committee members understand the context of peer review, how to interact with the audit firm concerning its peer review, and why the audit firm's peer review results should be important to an audit committee member. Peer review is required by AICPA membership requirements, most state boards of accountancy, and the Government Accountability Office (GAO) if a firm audits an organization that receives certain amounts of federal funding.

A peer review of a CPA firm can be used by an audit committee as a tool to assess whether the CPA firm it hires or is considering hiring

1. has a system of quality control for its accounting and auditing practice that has been designed to meet the requirements of the AICPA's Statements on Quality Control Standards (SQCSs), and
2. is complying with that system of quality control during the peer review year to provide the firm with reasonable assurance of complying with professional standards.

Peer reviews only include an evaluation of the CPA firm's non-SEC practice.

The AICPA's standards regarding quality control provide requirements in the quality control areas of auditor independence, integrity, and objectivity; audit personnel management; acceptance and continuance of audit clients and engagements; audit engagement performance; and firm quality control monitoring. Professional standards are literature, issued by various organizations, that contain the framework and rules that a CPA firm is expected to comply with when designing its quality control system and performing its work.

A CPA firm will engage another CPA firm to perform the peer review. However, the selected reviewer must be independent of the CPA firm, and must be qualified to perform the review and approved by the administering entity. This entity is the body responsible for administering, evaluating, and accepting peer reviews, and includes its peer review committee).

Peer Review Reports

The three types of peer review report opinions are pass, pass with deficiencies, or fail:

1. A *pass* report should be issued when it is concluded that the firm's system of quality control for the accounting and auditing practice has been suitably designed and was complied with to provide the firm with reasonable assurance of performing and reporting in conformity with applicable professional standards in all material respects.

2. A report rating of *pass with deficiencies* should be issued when the firm's system of quality control for the accounting and auditing practice has been suitably designed and complied with to provide the firm with reasonable assurance of performing and reporting with applicable professional standards in all material respects with the exception of a certain deficiency or deficiencies that are described in the report.

3. A report with a peer review rating of *fail* should be issued when significant deficiencies exist and the firm's system of quality control is not suitably designed to provide the firm with reasonable assurance of performing and reporting in conformity with applicable professional standards in all material respects, or the firm has not complied with its system of quality control to provide reasonable assurance of performing and reporting in conformity with applicable professional standards in all material respects.

If deficiencies are found, the firm is expected to identify and take corrective measures to prevent the same or similar types of deficiencies from occurring in the future. Such measures could include making appropriate changes in the firm's system of quality control or having personnel take additional continuing professional education courses in specified areas. These measures should be described in a letter addressed to the administering entity's peer review committee, responding to the deficiencies or significant deficiencies and related recommendations identified in the report. In reviewing the response to the deficiencies noted in the report, the peer review committee may ask the firm to agree to certain other actions (referred to as *corrective actions*) it deems appropriate in the circumstances, such as the submission of a monitoring report, a revisit by the reviewer, or joining an applicable audit quality center.

During the peer review, if a reviewer finds a matter that does not rise to the level of a deficiency, the reviewer will complete a Finding for Further Consideration (FFC) form. The reviewer will make a recommendation to the firm to correct the finding and the firm will be asked to respond. The administering entity's peer review committee will evaluate whether the reviewed firm's responses to those recommendations appear comprehensive, genuine, and feasible. The peer review committee will determine if a finding should require an implementation plan from the reviewed firm in addition to the plan described by the firm in its response to the findings on the FFC form.

We recommend that the company's audit committee request a copy of the auditor's most recently accepted peer review report and discuss these documents with the auditor. If a report receives a rating of *pass with deficiencies* or *fail*, the audit committee should discuss the reasons as part of its assessment of whether it should engage or continue to engage the auditor.

Common Misconceptions of Peer Review

1. *Fiction:* A peer review evaluates every engagement audited by a CPA firm.

   Fact: A peer review is performed using a risk-based approach. In addition to other procedures performed, a peer reviewer selects a reasonable cross-section of the firm's engagements so that the reviewer has a reasonable basis to determine whether the reviewed firm's system of quality is designed in accordance with professional standards and if the reviewed firm is in compliance with it. Therefore, it is possible that the review would not disclose all weaknesses in the system of quality control or all instances of lack of compliance with it.

2. *Fiction:* A *pass* rating provides assurance with respect to every engagement conducted by the firm.

   Fact: Every engagement conducted by a firm is not included in the scope of a peer review, nor is every aspect of each engagement reviewed. The peer review includes reviews of all key areas of engagements selected.

Questions for the Auditor Regarding Peer Review

The following questions are ones that the audit committee should consider asking its auditors in order to gain a better understanding of the firm's peer review experience.

Question	Yes	No	Comments
1. Has the firm previously or currently been subject to peer review? If not, please explain.	☐	☐	
2. Were there any deficiencies or finding for further consideration noted as part of the review? Explain what the deficiencies or findings mean.	☐	☐	
3. Does the firm's letter of response demonstrate that the firm is committed to making the changes necessary to improve its practice? If not, please explain.	☐	☐	
4. Was the peer review report a rating of pass with deficiencies or fail? Explain.	☐	☐	

(continued)

Question	Yes	No	Comments
5. Was our company's audit selected for review during the peer review? If so, were any matters from our audit noted? Explain.	☐	☐	
6. Did our audit's engagement partner (and/or other key engagement team members) have other audit engagements selected for review during the peer review? If so, were any matters noted?	☐	☐	

PCAOB Inspection

The Sarbanes-Oxley Act of 2002 (the Act) established the Public Company Accounting Oversight Board (PCAOB) to oversee the audits of issuers as defined in the Act. The PCAOB has established an inspection program to assess the degree of compliance of each registered public accounting firm and firm personnel with the Act. The PCAOB has also amended the Securities Exchange Act of 1934 to rest responsibility for the appointment, compensation, and oversight of any listed public company's auditor with a committee of independent directors. (PCAOB Release No. 2012-003, August 1, 2012)

All firms auditing public company clients are required to register with the PCAOB. Registered public accounting firms auditing more than 100 issuers are subject to inspection by the PCAOB on a yearly basis. All other registered firms are subject to an inspection every three years. The PCAOB inspection focuses on a firm's SEC practice only.

The PCAOB inspection focuses on the firm's audit practice with respect to SEC registrant organizations. Following the inspection, the PCAOB will issue a report in two parts: (1) a public report that includes a description of the inspection procedures and description of issues identified in the course of reviewing selected audit engagements without identification of the specific client engagements; and (2) a non-public report addressing criticisms of or potential defects in the firm's quality control system. The non-public report could be made public if the criticisms or defects are not addressed by the firm to the satisfaction of the PCAOB within 12 months of the date of the inspection report.

Questions for the Audit Committee Regarding the PCAOB Inspection

Although the PCAOB inspection does not include a firm's private company practice, it can still provide useful information to the audit committee of a private company. If the firm performs public company audits in addition to its private company audits, a PCAOB inspection report will be available. This report can provide insight about the firm in general, and the following questions are ones that the audit committee should consider asking its auditors.

Question	Yes	No	Comments
1. Did the PCAOB identify deficiencies in audits that involved auditing or accounting issues similar to issues presented in the company's audit?	☐	☐	
2. Has the firm taken actions necessary to correct the deficiencies noted? What was the audit firm's response to the PCAOB findings?	☐	☐	
3. Was the engagement partner (and other key engagement team members) selected for review? If so, were any negative comments noted on audits performed by them?	☐	☐	
4. Is the firm addressing (or has it addressed) the matters that were included in the non-public report from the PCAOB? Does the firm anticipate that the matters will be resolved, or is there a risk that the non-public report will become public after 12 months?	☐	☐	
5. Is there anything else of note related to the PCAOB inspection of which the audit committee should be aware?	☐	☐	

Chapter 7
Guidelines for Hiring the Chief Audit Executive (CAE)

> **Overview:** The internal audit function is a key component in providing assurance to the effectiveness of an organization's internal control structure. As a result, careful efforts must be taken in hiring the right chief audit executive (CAE), one who fits the company's needs with the necessary technical expertise, but also one who meets other requirements, such as industry experience, temperament, integrity, management and human relationship skills.
>
> **Background:** An internal audit function aids private company audit committees in carrying out their oversight and fiduciary responsibilities through its work to evaluate and improve internal control effectiveness. Audit committees should ensure that the company maintains an effective internal audit function. It must be noted that many small private companies cannot afford a full internal audit function. As a matter of best practices, a number of these smaller private companies contract with another CPA firm (independent of the firm engaged to perform the annual financial statement audit) or another independent service provider to administer periodic internal audit services in designated higher risk areas, rendering reports and discussing their findings with the audit committee.

Role of the Audit Committee in Hiring and Evaluating the CAE

In most companies, the CAE will report functionally to the audit committee and administratively to a senior executive of the company. This is a recommended best practice. A critical activity of the audit committee is to be involved in the hiring of the CAE of the company. Given the CAE's high degree of interaction with the audit committee, it is critical that the audit committee is comfortable working with this person.

CAE Qualifications

In general, candidates for a CAE position should have distinguished themselves professionally by earning either a CPA or a certified internal auditor (CIA) credential, or both, significant experience (10 years or more) in a management role, and strong technical skills in accounting and auditing. In addition, because of the breadth of experience it offers, the audit committee should seek candidates who have experience in audit, including but not limited to public accounting or its equivalent, and possibly an advanced business degree such as an MBA. It is strongly encouraged that all CAEs, either before appointment or within a reasonable time period after appointment, demonstrate a strong understanding of the roles and responsibilities of internal audit, the Institute of Internal Auditor's International Professional Practices Framework, and audit technical skills through attainment of the Certified Internal Auditor® (CIA®) designation.

When evaluating the qualifications of candidates for a CAE position, the following competencies should be considered:

- Ability to evaluate situations
- Good judgment
- Strength of character
- Business acumen and understanding of the organization's business
- Excellent verbal and written communication skills
- Critical thinking skills
- Excellent facilitation, problem-solving, and consensus building skills
- Highest level of ethics and integrity
- Ability to develop relationships with members of senior management
- Highest level of quality and professionalism
- Excellent people management skills

Instructions for this tool: The audit committee should consider asking the following questions of candidates who have passed the initial employment screening by either the company's human resources department or an outside recruiting firm. Note that some sample questions may not be appropriate for your organization or the candidate.

Chief Audit Executive—Sample Candidate Interview Questions	Interviewer Notes
1. What do you consider to be internal audit's role within the business?	
2. What do you see as the biggest challenges for an internal audit team in the short term (three to six months), medium term (six to 12 months), and over the next two to three years?	
3. Have you used technology in conducting internal audits, and how has it enhanced conducting the internal audit? Describe your experience with data analytics.	
4. What experience do you have in this industry, and how do you plan to keep abreast of the significant developments relevant to internal audit in this industry? What is your experience in addressing different business practices in different countries?	

Chief Audit Executive—Sample Candidate Interview Questions	Interviewer Notes
5. Have you worked with audit committees in the past? What processes have you put in place to keep the audit committee fully and appropriately informed? In the course of a year, what is the typical number of meetings/communications between the CAE and the audit committee (chair)?	
6. Give some examples of situations you have faced that required special meetings with the audit committee in executive session as a result of disagreements with management. How were these situations resolved with management? Have there been situations in which management has tried to squash your recommendations or discredit your findings, and what was your response? In retrospect, would you now handle these situations differently?	
7. Have you worked with the Committee of Sponsoring Organizations of the Treadway Commission (COSO) Internal Control Framework? How has the framework influenced your process in evaluating the adequacy of internal controls? How is this framework used to design your internal audits?	
8. In your previous company, what type of technology platform was used? Have you been involved in an enterprise resource planning (ERP) system implementation? What role did you play in the process and how did you make sure that the proper controls were in place when the system went live?	
9. Do you use a formal project planning process that is applied consistently for all internal audits? If so, what benefits have you derived in meeting your team's goals and objectives? What is your average report cycle time from the end of fieldwork?	
10. Have you ever conducted a formal risk assessment? How have you incorporated the results into setting up an audit plan?	

(continued)

Chief Audit Executive—Sample Candidate Interview Questions	Interviewer Notes
11. What roles do the organization's strategic and technology plans play in the development of an audit plan?	
12. Have you gone out to divisions, subsidiaries, or locations to ensure that they have significant input into audit objectives and scopes? How is this achieved? How have you resolved differences of opinion in this area without compromising the goals you have established for an audit?	
13. When you or your team conducts an internal audit, do you have a service orientation to your audit process? Do you work to improve the effectiveness and efficiency of the operations and controls in each audit area? How would you make your recommendations to management? What process would you use to resolve differences of opinion?	
14. Would you use a process for conducting a "customer satisfaction" survey after an internal audit is completed? How would you integrate this feedback into future audits?	
15. How would you ensure that the personnel in internal audit have the necessary skills to ensure an adequate understanding of divisional or departmental business?	
16. How many people have you managed, either as direct reports, or within an organization that you might have overseen? How would you describe your management style? Have you ever participated in a 360-degree assessment process? If so, what did you learn about yourself that surprised you? How did the results of the assessment change your behavior?	
17. Describe a situation in which you were able to use persuasion to convince someone to see things your way?	
18. Describe a situation where you came up with an innovative solution to a challenge your company was facing?	

Chief Audit Executive—Sample Candidate Interview Questions	Interviewer Notes
Other Notes and Questions:	

Chapter 8
Engaging Independent Counsel and Other Advisers

> **Overview:** An audit committee may need the expertise from outsiders other than the independent auditor. The tool in this chapter addresses the considerations to assist audit committee members in understanding the process of engaging independent counsel and other advisers if needed.

When selecting independent counsel or other advisers (expert or adviser) for an engagement within the company, the audit committee should not only consider the education, training, and experience of the specialists and staff assistants actually performing the work, but it should determine that the service provider (1) maintains integrity and objectivity; (2) is free of conflicts of interest with respect to the members of the audit committee and the company; (3) has the expertise and resources necessary to do the work it is under consideration to do; and (4) has a reputation for reliability, among other considerations.

Although the nature of every engagement will be different, the initial steps the audit committee (or its designee) should undertake when engaging external resources include the following:

1. Determine that the expert or adviser has the competence and experience to perform the requested service. Check references with other clients of the service provider.

2. Determine whether the expert or adviser has a conflict of interest with respect to the company. Such a conflict might arise if the expert or adviser has a relationship with the external auditor, or if he or she provides service to a competitor. Depending on the nature of the service to be offered, a conflict could arise if the expert or adviser has a relationship with a member of the board of directors, or a member of the company's management. Be aware of other potential conflicts of interest that may distract, or undermine, the work to be done.

3. Determine if the expert or adviser has sufficient resources to perform the work in the time frame specified by the audit committee.

4. Evaluate the scope of work to be performed and other issues, including the proposed plan for payment of fees and expenses.

5. Make sure all parties, including management and the expert or adviser, understand that the audit committee is the owner of the service relationship. Make sure that management understands that the expert or adviser is working on behalf of the audit committee and the audit committee expects management to be fully cooperative and forthcoming with respect to any information that may be requested.

6. Determine the criteria that will be used to measure the expert's/adviser's work and document those criteria in an agreement with the service provider.

7. Execute an engagement letter specifying the scope of services to be performed and the terms of the engagement.

As with any relationship, communication and expectations management are important.

PART II: Key Responsibilities

Chapter 9

Internal Control: Guidelines and Tool for the Audit Committee

> **Overview:** Overview: This chapter is intended to give audit committees basic information about internal control: to understand what it is, what it is not, how it can be used most effectively in the organization, and the requirements of management with respect to the system of internal control over financial reporting.

Internal Control Primer

In 1992, the Committee of Sponsoring Organizations (COSO)[1] of the National Commission on Fraudulent Financial Reporting, also known as the Treadway Commission, published a document called *Internal Control—Integrated Framework*.[2] The COSO *Framework* was cited as an example of a "suitable control framework" by the SEC, along with similar frameworks issued by Canadian and UK-based organizations, and has become widely used by US companies, both public and private. The COSO *Framework* was updated and re-published in 2013 to reflect consideration of the dramatic changes in business and operating environments since its original release. The framework now provides an updated and comprehensive principles-based approach to understanding internal control.

The COSO *Framework* defines internal control as "a process, effected by an entity's board of directors, management and other personnel, designed to provide reasonable assurance regarding the achievement of objectives relating to operations, reporting and compliance."

The COSO *Framework* sets forth three categories of objectives:

1. Operations Objectives pertain to the effectiveness and efficiency of the entity's operations, including operational and financial performance goals, and safeguarding assets against loss.

2. Reporting Objectives pertain to internal and external financial and non-financial reporting and may encompass reliability, timeliness, transparency, or other terms as set forth by regulators, standard setters, or the entity's policies.

3. Compliance Objectives pertain to adherence to laws and regulations to which the entity is subject.

---

[1] The Committee of Sponsoring Organizations consists of the American Institute of CPAs (AICPA), the Institute of Management Accountants (IMA), the Institute of Internal Auditors (IIA), Financial Executives International (FEI), and the American Accounting Association (AAA).

[2] The COSO publication *Internal Control—Integrated Framework* (Product Code Numbers 990025P and 990025E), may be purchased through the AICPA store at www.cpa2biz.com. The proceeds from the sale of the *Framework* are used to support the continuing work of COSO.

The COSO *Framework* states that internal control consists of five interrelated components as follows:

1. *Control environment.* The control environment is the set of standards, processes, and structures that provide the basis for carrying out internal control across the organization. The board of directors and senior management establish the tone at the top regarding the importance of internal control and expected standards of conduct

2. *Risk assessment.* Risk assessment involves a dynamic and iterative process for identifying and analyzing risks to achieving the entity's objectives, forming a basis for determining how risks should be managed. Management considers possible changes in the external environment and within its own business model that may impede the ability to achieve its objectives.

3. *Control activities.* Control activities are the actions established by policies and procedures to help ensure that management directives to mitigate risks related to the achievement of objectives are carried out. Control activities are performed at all levels of the entity and at various stages within business processes, and throughout the technology environment.

4. *Information and communication.* Information is necessary for the entity to carry out internal control responsibilities in support of achievement of its objectives. Communications occur both internally and externally, and provide the organization with the information needed to carry out day-to-day controls. Communication enables personnel to understand internal control responsibilities and their importance to the achievement of objectives.

5. *Monitoring Activities.* Ongoing evaluations, separate evaluations, or some combination of the two are used to ascertain whether each of the five components of internal control, including controls to effect the principles within each component, is present and functioning. Findings are evaluated and deficiencies are communicated in a timely manner, with serious matters reported to senior management and to the board.

The five components of internal control, along with seventeen principles representing the fundamental concepts associated with components, are linked together, forming an integrated system that can react dynamically to changing conditions. The internal control system is intertwined with the organization's operating activities, and is most effective when controls are built into the organization's infrastructure, becoming part of the very essence of the organization.

Internal Control Effectiveness

Internal control can be judged as effective if the board of directors and management has reasonable assurance of the following:

1. *Operations*—The organization
   - achieves effective and efficient operations when external events are considered unlikely to have a significant impact on the achievement of objectives or when the organization can reasonably predict the nature and timing of external events and mitigate the impact to an acceptable level; and

- understands the extent to which operations are managed effectively and efficiently when external events may have a significant impact on the achievement of objectives, and the impact cannot be mitigated to an acceptable level.

2. *Reporting*—The organization prepares reports in conformity with applicable laws, rules, regulations, and standards established by legislators, regulators, and standard setters, or with the entity's specified objectives and related policies.

3. *Compliance*—The organization complies with applicable laws, rules, and regulations.

What Internal Control Cannot Do

As important as an internal control structure is to an organization, an effective system is not a guarantee that the organization will be successful. An effective internal control structure will keep the right people informed about the organization's progress (or lack of progress) in achieving its objectives, but it cannot turn a poor manager into a good one. Internal control cannot ensure success, or even survival.

Internal control is not an absolute assurance to management and the board that the organization has achieved its objectives. It can only provide reasonable assurance, due to limitations inherent in all internal control systems. For example, breakdowns in the internal control structure can occur due to simple error or mistake, as well as faulty judgments that could be made at any level of management.

In addition, controls can be circumvented by collusion or by management override. Otherwise, effective internal controls cannot be relied upon to prevent, detect, or deter fraudulent financial reporting perpetrated by senior management. The audit committee must evaluate whether there are oversight mechanisms in place and functioning that will prevent, deter, or detect management override of internal controls.

Roles and Responsibilities

Everyone in the organization has some role to play in the organization's internal control system.

Board of Directors and Audit Committee

The board is responsible for overseeing the system of internal control, and plays a key role in setting expectations about integrity and ethical values, transparency, and accountability for the performance of internal control responsibilities. Board members should be objective, capable and inquisitive, with a willingness to commit the time necessary to fulfill their governance responsibilities. This is particularly important when the organization is controlled by an executive or management team with tight reins over the organization and the people within the organization. The board should recognize that its scope of oversight of the internal control system applies to all three major areas of control: operations, reporting, and compliance.

The audit committee plays a critical oversight role in the reliability of the financial statements, the system of internal control over financial reporting and the processes in place to design, implement, and monitor the company's broader system of internal control. Audit committee members should understand how management is carrying out its internal and external reporting responsibilities and verify that timely corrective actions are taken, as necessary.

Senior Management

Senior executives lead key operating units and business enabling functions and are a key influence on the design and implementation of internal controls that address related objectives.

CEO. The CEO has ultimate responsibility and ownership of the internal control system, with accountability to the board of directors. The individual in this role sets the tone at the top that affects the integrity and ethics and other factors that create the positive control environment needed for the internal control system to thrive. The CEO maintains visibility and control over the risks facing the entity, and reviews deficiencies that impact the system of internal control. The day-to-day design and operation of the control system is delegated to other senior managers in the company, under the leadership of the CEO.

CFO. Much of the internal control structure flows through the accounting and finance area of the organization under the leadership of the CFO. In particular, controls over financial reporting fall within the domain of the chief financial officer. The audit committee should use interactions with the CFO as one of several important factors in the basis for their comfort level on the completeness, accuracy, validity, and maintenance of the system of internal control over financial reporting.

In a private company, the CFO and CEO should, among other things, set the appropriate "tone at the top" for the organization's control environment by doing the following:

- Ensuring that executives and management at all levels of the organization understand their role in cultivating the proper level of control awareness and play an integral part in establishing and maintaining internal controls
- Mandating accountability through properly established policies and procedures and monitoring compliance on an ongoing basis
- Designing internal controls so that risks are effectively managed and that material weaknesses are identified and reported to the appropriate level of management in a timely manner
- Requiring disclosure to the company's auditors and the audit committee of (a) all significant deficiencies in the design or operation of internal controls that could adversely affect the company's ability to record, process, summarize, and report financial data, as well as any material weaknesses in internal control; and (b) any fraud, whether or not material, that involves management or other employees who have a significant role in the company's internal controls
- Requiring that annual financial reports indicate whether or not there were significant changes in internal controls or in other factors that could significantly affect internal controls subsequent to the date of evaluation, including any corrective actions with regard to significant deficiencies and material weaknesses

Business-Enabling Functions

Certain functions exist to support the organization through specialized skills such as finance, risk management, information technology, and human resources. These functions also monitor trends, provide guidance, and keep the organization informed of relevant requirements as important internal controls. Coordination and sharing of issues among these functions help the organization achieve its objectives.

Controller. Much of the basics of the control system come under the domain of this position. It is key that the controller understand the need for the internal control system, is committed to the system, and communicates the importance of the system to all people in the accounting organization. Further, the controller must demonstrate respect for the system though his or her actions.

Internal Audit

A main role for the internal audit team is to evaluate the effectiveness of the internal control system and contribute to its ongoing effectiveness. With the internal audit team reporting directly to the audit committee of the board of directors and the most senior levels of management, it is often this function that plays a significant role in monitoring the effectiveness of the internal control system.

External Parties

Third parties frequently play key roles in a company's activities through outsourcing or other support. The company retains full responsibility for the internal control system, including activities performed by third parties on its behalf. Therefore, the audit committee should ensure that management has processes to evaluate the activities performed by others to assess the effectiveness of the third party's system of internal control.

External Audit. The external auditor is engaged to audit the reliability of financial reporting and, in certain reporting jurisdictions, the effectiveness of internal control over financial reporting. In carrying out these responsibilities, the external auditor will communicate deficiencies in internal control to management to be acted upon and, depending on significance, to the audit committee.

All Other Personnel

The internal control system is only as effective as the employees throughout the organization who must comply with it. Employees throughout the organization should understand their roles in internal control, the importance of supporting the system through their own actions, and encouraging respect for the system by their colleagues throughout the organization.

Internal Control Over Financial Reporting

All SEC reporting companies are subject to the Sarbanes-Oxley Act of 2002 (the Act). Under Section 404 of the Act, management is responsible for maintaining a system of internal control over financial reporting (ICFR). Management is also required to evaluate annually whether ICFR is effective at providing reasonable assurance and disclose the results of that evaluation to investors.

While this examination is not applicable to private companies, many have voluntarily adopted and established processes to adhere to Section 404 of the Act as the enhanced governance benefit that results is extended to owners, banks, and other related parties. Continued adoption is expected, particularly for private companies that establish goals towards becoming a public company where compliance will be mandatory. The AICPA's publication *Audit Committee Toolkit: Public Companies* can assist companies of all sizes in better understanding the requirements.

All audit committees should become familiar with ICFR concepts as matters related to internal control over financial reporting will be included in external auditor communications to the audit committee[3] as part of expressing or disclaiming an opinion on financial statements.

Key Terms in Internal Control Over Financial Reporting Control

There are a few terms that you will hear frequently when discussing internal control, and these are identified and described as follows:

Entity-level controls. Several types of entity-level controls influence ICFR, including the following:

- Controls related to the control environment
- Controls over management override
- The company's risk assessment process
- Centralized processing and controls, including shared service environments
- Controls to monitor results of operations
- Controls to monitor other controls, including activities of the internal audit function, the audit committee, and self-assessment programs
- Controls over the period-end financial reporting process
- Policies that address significant business control and risk management practices

Compensating controls. A primary means of addressing potential concerns about limited segregation of duties, compensating controls include managers reviewing system reports of detailed transactions; selecting transactions for review of supporting documents; overseeing periodic counts of physical inventory, equipment, or other assets and comparing them with accounting records; and reviewing reconciliations of account balances or performing them independently. The lack of segregation of duties is not automatically a material weakness, or even a significant deficiency, depending on the compensating controls that are in place.

Control Deficiency. The design or operation of a control does not allow management or employees, in the normal course of performing their assigned functions, to prevent or detect misstatements on a timely basis.

---

[3] AU sec. 325, *Communicating Internal Control Related Matters Identified in an Audit.*

Example: A member of the accounting department has been assigned responsibility to perform reconciliations on all bank accounts on a monthly basis. This person also has responsibility for opening the mail and preparing the daily deposit to the bank. The person's manager is required to review each reconciliation when completed, but the manager does not sign off consistently on the reconciliation indicating review. Two internal control deficiencies exist here: (1) the lack of segregation of duties because one individual is preparing the cash deposit and reconciling the cash accounts, and (2) the lack of documentation of a control because the manager does not evidence review so it is not clear that the review has been performed.

Significant Deficiency. A deficiency, or a combination of deficiencies, in internal control over financial reporting that is less severe than a material weakness, yet important enough to merit attention by those responsible for oversight of the company's financial reporting. Alone or with other deficiencies, this type of control deficiency results in more than a remote likelihood that a misstatement of the financials that is more than inconsequential in amount will not be prevented or detected.

Example: The company uses a standard sales contract, making it necessary for the accounting department to review completed sales contracts for changes to standard shipping terms to assure the proper timing for recognizing revenue from sales. Because the terms are not always reviewed, revenue has been overstated on occasion. It is unlikely that any single sales contract could result in a material overstatement of revenue, and there are controls in place to ensure that materials misstatements do not occur. However, a misstatement that is more than inconsequential yet less than material could result, creating a significant deficiency in internal control.

Material Weakness. A deficiency, or a combination of deficiencies, in internal control over financial reporting, such that there is a reasonable possibility that a material misstatement of the company's annual or interim financial statements will not be prevented or detected and corrected on a timely basis.

Examples of weaknesses that likely would be considered material depending on the circumstances include the following:

- Ineffective oversight by the audit committee over the external financial reporting process, and the internal controls over financial reporting
- Material misstatements in the financial statements not identified initially by the company's internal controls
- Significant deficiencies that have been communicated to management and the audit committee but that remain uncorrected after a reasonable period of time
- Restatement of previously issued financial statements to correct a material misstatement
- For larger, more complex entities, ineffective internal audit functions
- For complex entities in highly regulated industries, ineffective regulatory compliance function
- Fraud of any magnitude on the part of senior management
- An ineffective control environment

The severity of a deficiency depends on two factors: (1) whether there is a reasonable possibility that the company's controls will fail to prevent or detect a misstatement of an account balance or disclosure, and (2) the magnitude of the potential misstatement resulting from the deficiency or deficiencies. It is important to state that the severity of a deficiency does not depend on whether a misstatement actually occurred but rather on whether there is a reasonable possibility that the company's controls will fail to prevent or detect a misstatement. In determining whether a deficiency rises to the level of resulting in a misstatement of an account balance, risk factors need to be considered. These risk factors include, but are not limited to the following:

- The nature of the financial statement accounts, disclosures, and assertions involved
- The susceptibility of the related assets or liability to loss or fraud
- The subjectivity, complexity, or extent of judgment required to determine the amount involved
- The interaction or relationship of the control with other controls, including whether they are interdependent or redundant
- The interaction of the deficiencies
- The possible future consequences of the deficiency

For additional guidance, refer to AU section 325 section titled "Evaluating Deficiencies Identified as Part of an Audit."

ICFR Results

The audit committee needs to be advised and updated regularly on the external auditor's consideration of internal control as part of the financial statement audit, and should have a clear understanding of the expected outcome. In the event the auditor identifies internal control deficiencies, management should have a plan already in place to correct the weakness(es), and the audit committee should already be engaged in review and approval of that plan.

Conclusion

This primer is intended to provide an overview of what is meant by internal control, key terms, concepts, and responsibilities of the audit committee, especially as they relate to internal control over financial reporting. The concepts are not complex, but sometimes the application of internal control can be a challenge in an organization, depending on its size and the corporate culture. The audit committee plays an important role in establishing an appropriate control environment or the tone at the top of the organization.

While the objective of reliable financial reporting may be paramount for the audit committee of a private company, an effective internal control system also encompasses compliance, operational, and non-financial reporting objectives. An integrated process that includes all five components of the internal control framework and its 17 principles working together is the primary means of having reasonable assurance that these important goals are being met. Simply stated, at the end of the day, a strong system of internal control, both in its design and operation, is good business.

Internal Control—Checklist of COSO Essentials for the Board

Purpose of this tool: This tool provides an understanding of key board-level responsibilities within each of the five interrelated components of a company's internal control system, as described in the *COSO Internal Control—Integrated Framework (2013)*. Refer to the "Internal Control Primer" section of this chapter for a discussion of the COSO components. The audit committee's role within this system focuses on internal controls over financial reporting and the processes in place to design, implement, and monitor the company's broader system of internal control. It is also responsible to aid the board in its oversight of internal controls, risk management and overall governance process. This can be achieved through the committee's interaction with senior management, independent auditors, internal auditors, and other key members of the financial management team.

Instructions for using this tool: Within each component is a series of questions that the audit committee should evaluate to assure itself that board-level controls are in place and functioning. These questions should be discussed in an open forum with the individuals who have a basis for responding to the questions. The audit committee should ask for detailed answers and examples from the management team, which should include key members of the financial management team, internal auditors, and independent auditors. **This board-level tool should be used in conjunction with the COSO *Internal Control—Integrated Framework* (2013) to determine if all components and related principles of a company's internal control system are present, functioning, and operating together in an integrated manner.** Evaluation of the internal control structure is not a one-time event, but rather a continuous process for the audit committee—the audit committee should always have its eyes and ears open to the ever-changing risks that the business faces, especially the risks to reliable financial reporting, and should continually probe the responsible parties regarding the operation of the system and potential weaknesses in internal control. These questions are written in such a manner that a "No" response indicates a weakness that must be addressed.

COSO Framework	Yes	No	Not sure	Comments
Control Environment—Demonstrates Commitment to Integrity and Ethical Values				
1. Do comprehensive standards of conduct exist addressing acceptable business practice, conflicts of interest, and expected standards of ethical and moral behavior for the company? Is the board accountable for the definition and application of the standards?	☐	☐	☐	
2. Is the audit committee furnished routinely with the results of employee surveys regarding corporate behavior and similar information from external parties such as customers and vendors? See also chapter 10, "Fraud and the Responsibilities of the Audit Committee: An Overview," in this toolkit.	☐	☐	☐	
3. Are the standards of conduct communicated and reinforced regularly to all levels of the organization, outsourced service providers, and business partners? Are management's efforts to communicate the standards both sufficient and effective in creating awareness and motivating compliance? See also chapter 10, "Fraud and the Responsibilities of the Audit Committee: An Overview," in this toolkit.	☐	☐	☐	
4. Do the board and management demonstrate through actions and behaviors their commitment to the standards of conduct? Is there consistency at all levels of the organization?	☐	☐	☐	

COSO Framework	Yes	No	Not sure	Comments
Control Environment—Exercises Oversight Responsibility				
5. Does the board of directors define, maintain, and evaluate periodically the skills and expertise needed among its members to enable them to ask probing questions of senior management and take commensurate actions?	☐	☐	☐	
6. Does the board set the expectations for the performance, integrity, and ethical values of the chief executive officer (or equivalent role)?	☐	☐	☐	
7. Does the board assume oversight responsibility for management's design, implementation, and conduct of internal control?	☐	☐	☐	
Control Environment—Establishes Structure, Authority, and Responsibility				
8. Has the board established appropriate oversight structures and processes (i.e. board and committees) for the entity?	☐	☐	☐	
9. Does the board retain authority over significant decisions and review management's assignments and limitations of authorities and responsibilities?	☐	☐	☐	
Control Environment—Demonstrates Commitment to Competence				
10. Do board committees contain members who have the requisite level of skills and expertise commensurate with the committee's responsibilities?	☐	☐	☐	
11. Are board oversight effectiveness reviews commissioned periodically, with opportunities for improvement identified and addressed?	☐	☐	☐	
12. Is the board effective in exercising its fiduciary responsibilities to shareholders or other owners (as applicable) and due care in oversight (for example, prepare for and attend meetings, review the entity's financial statements and other disclosures)?	☐	☐	☐	

(continued)

COSO Framework	Yes	No	Not sure	Comments
Control Environment—Demonstrates Commitment to Competence				
13. Does the board evaluate the performance, integrity and ethical values of the chief executive officer (or equivalent role) and act as necessary to address shortcomings?	☐	☐	☐	
14. Do succession plans, contingency plans, or both exist for the CEO and other key roles in order to assign responsibilities important to internal control?	☐	☐	☐	
Control Environment—Enforces Accountability				
15. Does the board challenge senior management by asking probing questions about the entity's plans and performance, and require follow-up and corrective actions, as necessary?	☐	☐	☐	
16. Does the board act to address competence, internal control, and standards of conduct shortcomings among the CEO, the organization, and its outsourced service providers?	☐	☐	☐	
17. Does the board align executive compensation, incentives, and rewards appropriately, including consideration of related pressures, with the fulfillment of internal control responsibilities in the achievement of objectives?	☐	☐	☐	
Risk Assessment				
1. Does the board consider significant risks to the achievement of objectives from external sources, such as creditor demands, economic conditions, regulation, labor relations, and sustainability? Does the organization identify related issues and trends?	☐	☐	☐	

COSO Framework	Yes	No	Not sure	Comments
Risk Assessment				
2. Does the organization consider significant risks to the achievement of objectives from internal sources, such as business continuity, retention of and succession planning for key employees, financing and the availability of funding for key programs, competitive compensation and benefits, and information systems security and backup systems? Does the organization identify related issues and trends?	☐	☐	☐	
3. Does management have a process in place to assess risk proactively as significant changes, such as entering a new market, disruptive innovations, economic/geopolitical shifts, fraud, and management override of internal controls, occur?	☐	☐	☐	
4. Does the board apply an appropriate level of skepticism and challenge management's assessment of risks?	☐	☐	☐	
Control Activities				
1. Does the board assume the responsibility to oversee senior management effectively in its performance of control activities?	☐	☐	☐	
2. Does the board have necessary assurance from management, internal and external auditors, and others (as appropriate) that control activities are designed effectively and operating to address all significant risks to the preparation of reliable financial statements?	☐	☐	☐	

(continued)

COSO Framework	Yes	No	Not sure	Comments
Control Activities				
3. Does the board make specific inquiries of management regarding the selection, development, and deployment of control activities in significant risk areas and remediation as necessary? Does the company design control activities proactively to address emerging significant risk areas?	☐	☐	☐	
Information and Communication				
1. Do the board and management have an effective level of communications in place to enable fulfillment of their roles with respect to the entity's objectives and to enable consistency in direction and tone at the top?	☐	☐	☐	
2. Does the board receive the necessary operational and financial information relating to the entity's achievement of objectives on a timely basis and in a format that facilitates its use? Does the board review and discuss this information?	☐	☐	☐	
3. Does the board apply critical judgment effectively to scrutinize information provided and present alternative views?	☐	☐	☐	
4. Does the board review disclosures to external stakeholders for completeness, relevance, and accuracy?	☐	☐	☐	
5. Does the board receive communications regarding relevant information from third party assessments?	☐	☐	☐	
6. Do open communication channels exist to allow relevant information to flow to the board from customers, consumers, suppliers, external auditors, regulators, financial analysts, and others?	☐	☐	☐	

COSO Framework	Yes	No	Not sure	Comments
Information and Communication				
7. Is there an effective process established and publicized periodically to officers, employees, and others to allow open communication of suspected instances of wrongdoing by the company or employees of the company? See also the tool titled "Whistle-blower Common Practices Checklist" in chapter 11, "Whistleblower Policy: Complaint Reporting Procedures and Tracking Report," in this toolkit.	☐	☐	☐	
Monitoring Activities				
1. Does the board understand the nature and scope of ongoing monitoring procedures and/or separate evaluations to enable an effective evaluation of whether the components of internal control continue to function over time?	☐	☐	☐	
2. Does the board inquire with management, internal and external auditors, and others (as appropriate) to understand the presence and nature of any management overrides of controls?	☐	☐	☐	
3. Does the board receive regular communications from management regarding its evaluation of internal control and the status of remediation of deficiencies?	☐	☐	☐	
4. Does the board engage with management, internal and external auditors, and others (as appropriate) to evaluate the adaptability of the company's strategies and internal control framework to evolving business, infrastructure, regulations, and other factors?	☐	☐	☐	

Chapter 10
Fraud and the Responsibilities of the Audit Committee: An Overview

> **Overview:** An audit committee should take an active role in the prevention and deterrence of fraud, in addition to implementing and maintaining an effective ethics and compliance program. Effective audit committees challenge management constantly, and the auditors should take steps continually to ensure that the entity has appropriate antifraud programs and controls in place. With those controls, management will be able to identify potential fraud and undertake investigations when instances of fraud are detected. The audit committee should take an interest in ensuring that appropriate action is taken against known perpetrators of fraud.
>
> This chapter is intended to make audit committee members, including board members and other oversight committees within the private sector, aware of their responsibilities as they undertake this important role. This chapter highlights areas of corporate activity that may require additional scrutiny by the audit committee.

Since the passage of the Sarbanes-Oxley Act of 2002, the public's expectations have been raised about all parties involved in organizational governance, including the audit committee, management, independent auditors, internal auditors, regulators, and law enforcement. The audit committee's role has been elevated greatly as a result of such fraud discoveries and by recent legislation and new stock exchange requirements.

Regulations such as the U.S. Foreign Corrupt Practices Act of 1977 (FCPA), the 1997 Organisation for Economic Co-operation and Development Anti-Bribery Convention, the U.S. Sarbanes-Oxley Act of 2002, the U.S. Federal Sentencing Guidelines of 2005, and similar legislation throughout the world have increased management's responsibility for fraud risk management.[1]

Definition and Categories of Fraud

An understanding of fraud is essential for the audit committee to carry out its responsibilities. According to *Black's Law Dictionary* (Tenth Edition, 2014, p.775), *fraud*

> ... a knowing misrepresentation or knowing concealment of a material fact made to induce another to act to his or her detriment. A reckless misinterpretation made without justified belief in its truth to induce another person to act. Additional elements in a claim for fraud may include reasonable reliance on the misrepresentation and damages resulting from this reliance. Unconscionable dealing; the unfair use of the power arising out of the parties' relative positions and resulting in an unconscionable bargain... consists of some deceitful practice or willful device, resorted to with intent to deprive another of his right, or in some

---

[1] IIA, AICPA, ACFE. "Managing the Business Risk of Fraud: A Practical Guide." 2008, p. 5.

manner to do him an injury. As distinguished from negligence, it is always positive, intentional.... Fraud, in the sense of a court of equity, properly includes all acts, omissions, and concealments which involve a breach of legal or equitable duty, trust, or confidence justly reposed, and are injurious to another, or by which an undue and unconscientious advantage is taken of another.[2]

The AICPA defines *fraud* as "an intentional act by one or more individuals among management, those charged with governance, employees, or third parties, involving the use of deception that results in a misstatement in financial statements that are the subject of an audit."[3]

Fraud affecting the organization generally falls within one of three categories:

1. *Financial statement fraud*, where an employee intentionally causes a misstatement or omission of material information in the organization's financial reports (for example, recording fictitious revenues, understating reported expenses or artificially inflating reported assets).

2. *Corruption*, where an employee misuses his or her influence in a business transaction in a way that violates his or her duty to the employer in order to gain a direct or indirect benefit, such as schemes involving bribery or conflicts of interest.

3. *Asset misappropriation*, where an employee steals or misuses the organization's resources (for example, theft of company cash, false billing schemes or inflated expense reports).

These fraud schemes can arise from the following sources within a company:

- *Executive fraud*, which involves senior management's intentional misrepresentation of financial statements, or theft or improper use of company resources.

- *Management fraud*, which involves middle management's intentional misrepresentation of financial statement transactions, for example, to improve their apparent performance.

- *Employee fraud*, which involves non senior employee theft or improper use of company resources.

- *External fraud*, which involves theft or improper use of resources by people who are neither management nor employees of the firm. Outside individuals may, for example, collude with management or employees.

Roles of the Audit Committee in the Prevention, Deterrence, Investigation, and Discovery or Detection of Fraud

The members of the audit committee should understand their role of ensuring that the organization has a strong internal control environment in place, including the design and implementation of programs and controls to prevent and detect fraud. The audit committee also needs to be prepared to aid in the discovery of fraud, investigate, and report on its findings to the board. The components of a robust fraud control program should include a fraud risk

---

[2] Black's Law Dictionary: thelawdictionary.org/fraud/

[3] www.aicpa.org/research/standards/auditattest/downloadabledocuments/au-c-00240.pdf

assessment,[4] fraud reporting mechanisms and protocols, investigation protocols, a disciplinary action policy applied consistently, and a process to identify and report conflicts of interest, usually in the form of an annual conflict of interest questionnaire completed by all employees.

The audit committee should ensure that the organization has implemented an effective ethics and compliance program, and that it is tested periodically. The design of the internal control system should consider the risk of fraud explicitly. Since the occurrence of significant frauds can be attributed frequently to an override of internal controls, the audit committee plays an important role by validating the accuracy of information received by applying skepticism and ensuring that internal controls both address the appropriate risk areas and are functioning as designed. Sarbanes-Oxley section 301 requires audit committees of listed companies to establish procedures for the receipt, retention, and treatment of complaints received by the issuer regarding accounting, internal accounting controls, or auditing matters; and the confidential, anonymous submission by employees of the issuer of concerns regarding questionable accounting or auditing matters. Private companies should consider this guidance for establishing similar policies and procedures.[5] See also the tool in chapter 11, "Whistleblower Policy: Complaint Reporting Procedures and Tracking Report," in this toolkit.

Governance Considerations

To set the appropriate tone at the top, the board of directors should first ensure that the board itself is governed properly. This encompasses all aspects of board governance, including independent-minded board members who exercise control over board information, agenda, and access to management and outside advisers, and who independently carry out the responsibilities of the nominating/governance, compensation, audit, and other committees.

The board also has the responsibility to ensure that management designs effective fraud risk management documentation to encourage ethical behavior and to empower employees, customers, and vendors to insist those standards are met every day. The board should do the following:

- Understand fraud risks.
- Maintain oversight of the fraud risk assessment by ensuring that fraud risk has been considered as part of the organization's risk assessment and strategic plans. This responsibility should be addressed under a periodic agenda item at board meetings when general risks to the organization are considered.
- Monitor management's reports on fraud risks, policies, and control activities, which include obtaining assurance that the controls are effective. The board should also establish mechanisms to ensure it is receiving accurate and timely information from management, employees, internal and external auditors, and other stakeholders regarding potential fraud occurrences.

---

[4] The COSO publication *Internal Control—Integrated Framework*, Principle 8, (page 78) describes the assessment of fraud risk as one of the fundamental concepts of internal control within an organization.

[5] *See also* IIA, AICPA, ACFE. "Managing the Business Risk of Fraud: A Practical Guide." 2008, p. 11, for guidance regarding the roles of management and staff.

- Oversee the internal controls established by management.
- Set the appropriate tone at the top through the CEO job description, hiring, evaluation, and succession-planning processes.
- Have the ability to retain and pay outside experts where needed.
- Provide external auditors with evidence regarding the board's active involvement and concern about fraud risk management.

The board may choose to delegate oversight of some or all of such responsibilities to a committee of the board. These responsibilities should be documented in the board and applicable committee charters. The board should ensure it has sufficient resources of its own and approve sufficient resources in the budget and long-range plans to enable the organization to achieve its fraud risk management objectives.

Expertise of Forensic Accounting Consultants

In some situations, it may be necessary for an organization to look beyond the independent audit team for expertise in the fraud area. In such cases, CPA and CFE forensic accounting consultants can provide additional assurance or advanced expertise, since they have special training and experience in fraud prevention, deterrence, investigation, and detection. Forensic accounting consultants may also provide fresh insights into the organization's operations, control systems, and risks. The work of forensic accounting consultants may also provide comfort for the organization's CEO and CFO, who are required to file certifications under Sarbanes-Oxley. Forensic accounting consultants, however, cannot act as insurers to prevent or detect fraud.

When Fraud Is Discovered

Fraud can be discovered through many sources, including internal or external auditors, forensic accounting consultants, employees, and vendors. Establishing a confidential hotline can also be an important source of information leading to fraud discovery, as part of an organization's overall ethics, compliance, and fraud prevention program.

If fraud or improprieties are asserted or discovered, the audit committee—through the external auditors, internal auditors, forensic accounting consultants, or others as appropriate—should investigate, and, if necessary, retain legal counsel to assert claims on the organization's behalf. See the tool in chapter 8, "Engaging Independent Counsel and Other Advisers," in this toolkit. Forensic accounting consultants, in particular, may be needed to provide the depth of skills necessary to conduct a fraud investigation, and if it is desirable, to get an independent assessment.

If fraud is discovered, or there is a reasonable basis to believe that fraud may have occurred, the audit committee is responsible for ensuring that an investigation is undertaken. Criteria should be in place describing the audit committee's level of involvement, based on the severity of the offense. Audit committees will also want to obtain information about all violations of the law and the organization's policies.

Forensic accounting consultants frequently can also provide audit committees with other related advisory services, namely, (1) evaluations of controls designs and operating effectiveness through compliance verification; (2) creation of special investigations units (SIUs); (3) incident management committees; (4) disclosure risk controls; and (5) ethics hotlines and a code of conduct, if they are not already in place.

The audit committee can engage the incumbent audit firm to carry out a forensic/fraud investigation. It is important to recognize, however, that the audit firm would be precluded from serving subsequently as an expert witness in such circumstances. Audit committees should therefore consider the use of forensic professionals who are not affiliated with the audit firm, since they would not be subject to such constraints. If fraud is discovered and an investigation is necessary, the company's general counsel or an outside law firm should be engaged to determine how best to proceed with the investigation. In addition, if CPA forensic accountants are engaged by the corporate office of general counsel, rather than the audit committee, they may attain attorney-client privilege status potentially, which is not otherwise available under normal circumstances.

Conclusion

Reactions to recent corporate scandals have led the public and stakeholders to expect organizations to take a "no fraud tolerance" attitude. Good governance principles demand that an organization's board of directors, or equivalent oversight body, ensure overall high ethical behavior in the organization, regardless of its status as public, private, government, or not-for-profit; its relative size; or its industry. The board's role is critically important because major frauds have historically been perpetrated by senior management in collusion with other employees. Vigilant handling of fraud cases within an organization sends a clear signal to the public, stakeholders, and regulators about the board and management's attitude toward fraud risks and about the organization's fraud risk tolerance. Independent public accountants, hired by audit committees, and internal auditors will continue to play an important part in the process. CPA forensic accounting consultants have emerged, however, as vital recognized allies. Qualified forensic accounting consultants have the education, training, and experience to provide additional assistance to audit committees so that they may carry out their fiduciary responsibilities more effectively in the fight against fraud.

Chapter 11
Whistleblower Policy: Complaint Reporting Procedures and Tracking Report*

> **Overview:** Audit committees of many private companies employ a process to review any complaints received by the company, whether generated internally or externally, regarding internal accounting controls or auditing matters. While not a compliance mandate as it is for public companies, an effective whistleblower policy and process is part of strong corporate governance by providing a means to address unethical or illegal activity.

Reasons for Tool

The Sarbanes-Oxley Act of 2002 (the Act) includes a number of provisions that affect audit committees of public companies and their response to complaints regarding financial fraud. Section 301 of the Act contains whistleblower provisions that require audit committees to establish procedures for the reporting of complaints including "(*a*) the receipt, retention, and treatment of complaints received by the issuer regarding accounting, internal accounting controls, or auditing matters; and (*b*) the confidential, anonymous submission by employees of the issuer regarding questionable accounting or auditing matters."

In addition, Section 802 of the Act prohibits retaliation by a publicly traded company against whistleblowers in securities fraud cases, and creates a private right of action for aggrieved employees. Various other state and federal laws relating to reporting of criminal activity and fraud contain provisions that protect whistleblowers from retaliation. In 2013, the U.S. Supreme Court ruled[1] that whistleblower protections of Section 802 are extended to also shield private companies and subcontractors who perform work for public companies; thus employee concerns that may be covered under the Act's whistleblower provisions should be handled with care.

The Dodd-Frank Act's Section 922, which became effective in 2011, adds further protections for private company whistleblowers who provide the SEC with original information regarding a potential violation of federal securities laws (for example, seeking investors). It creates monetary awards for eligible whistleblowers and provides the means for information to be reported anonymously and directly to the SEC.

A vigorous whistleblowing process is a company's key defense against management override. The audit committee can assist in creating strong antifraud controls by encouraging the development of a culture in which employees view whistleblowing as a valuable contribution

---

* Note: This tool is included for illustrative purposes only. It has not been considered or acted upon by any senior technical committee or the AICPA Board of Directors and does not represent an official opinion or position of the AICPA. It is provided with the understanding that the author and publisher are not engaged in rendering legal, accounting, or other professional service. If legal advice or other expert assistance is required, the services of a competent professional should be sought.
[1] U.S. Code 18 U.S.C. §1514A, *Whistleblower Protection for Employees of Publicly Traded Companies.*

to an attractive workplace of integrity and their own futures. The reporting mechanisms must demonstrate confidentiality so potential whistleblowers are assured that their concerns will be considered properly, and that they will not be subjected to retribution. Successful whistleblowing procedures require strong leadership from the audit committee, the board of directors, and management.

The audit committee plays a key role in assuring that employees are encouraged to report illegal or excessively risky activity internally, are confident in the process to investigate concerns, and are protected from retaliation. Prompt self-reporting of potential violations to the SEC may be considered when a company finds credible evidence during its internal investigation.

Whistleblower Common Practices Checklist

Purpose of this tool: This tool contains a checklist of issues for audit committees to consider when evaluating the design and operating effectiveness of the whistleblower process. These questions are written in a manner such that a "No" response indicates areas where additional thought or action is recommended for an effective program.

	Yes	No	Not sure	Comments
Policy Components				
1. Has a whistleblower policy been developed and communicated to employees and external service providers?	☐	☐	☐	
2. Does the policy describe the following:	☐	☐	☐	
a. A statement of purpose and the nature of concerns within the policy's scope? Does the policy support and clarify how it differs from the company's normal complaint procedures?				
b. The parties involved in the receipt, handling, and disposition of complaints, including the audit committee?	☐	☐	☐	
c. The reporting obligations of employees and external service providers, as well as timeliness expectations?	☐	☐	☐	
d. The communication channels available for reporting a concern?	☐	☐	☐	
e. Confidentiality safeguards that an individual who makes a report can expect?	☐	☐	☐	
f. The steps to follow in order to make an anonymous report, as well as the related handling procedures?	☐	☐	☐	

(continued)

	Yes	No	Not sure	Comments
Policy Components				
g. The definition of good faith, credible reporting? Does the policy address the handling of vague complaints received from an anonymous source?	☐	☐	☐	
h. The steps used to receive, investigate, and track reported issues?	☐	☐	☐	
i. The retention requirement for whistleblower complaints?	☐	☐	☐	
j. Whistleblower protections, unacceptable retaliatory actions, the process to report retaliation, and the process the company will use to investigate suspected retaliation?	☐	☐	☐	
k. Procedures that board-level directors should follow to make a complaint?	☐	☐	☐	
3. Is the policy publicized widely and recommunicated periodically so that all employees and service providers have awareness?	☐	☐	☐	
Procedural Components				
1. Is more than one communication channel available to employees, such as telephone, web, or email? Do channels have sufficient ease of use and provide for confidentiality and anonymity?	☐	☐	☐	
Procedural Components				
2. Are the communication channels that an issue must flow through before reaching the board effective in assuring that financial reporting issues reach the audit committee for evaluation consistently?	☐	☐	☐	
3. Is there a mechanism in place that assures automatic submission of any issue involving senior management directly to the audit committee without filtering?	☐	☐	☐	

	Yes	No	Not sure	Comments
Procedural Components				
4. Is there a process that allows an individual to receive information about the disposition of their report at an appropriate level?	☐	☐	☐	
5. Are issues investigated and resolved in a timely manner?	☐	☐	☐	
6. Are all issues received through whistleblower communication channels documented, tracked, and reported to the audit committee for discussion?	☐	☐	☐	
7. Are all issues that reach the audit committee documented, tracked until completion, and maintained per the retention policy?	☐	☐	☐	
8. Does the audit committee have a robust process in place to evaluate reported issues where supporting evidence is found for potential self-disclosure to the SEC?	☐	☐	☐	
9. Are internal audits performed regularly on the whistleblower program to assure the design and operating effectiveness of the defined protocols?	☐	☐	☐	

Sample Procedures For Handling Complaints (Whistleblower Policy)

Purpose of this tool: This tool could be used by the audit committee and management to state the policy, procedures, and the confidentiality requirements that a person with a complaint should follow to report and track complaints received to an appropriate resolution.

Statement of Purpose

The corporation strives to conduct all of its activities according to high ethical standards. Adherence to this goal is imperative in connection with the preparation of the corporation's financial statements. The audit committee of the corporation's board of directors has adopted these procedures for handling complaints to assist the corporation in meeting its ethical and legal obligations in connection with its accounting and auditing practices.

Employee Complaints

The corporation encourages any employee who has a concern regarding what he or she views as a questionable accounting or auditing practice to bring this concern to the attention of the audit committee. Generally, such concerns should be raised initially with the individuals involved in the preparation and review of the corporation's financial reports; however, if an employee is unsuccessful in resolving a concern through such channels or believes that the concern will not be adequately addressed through such channels, the employee should contact a member of the audit committee.

The names of the current members of the audit committee and the phone number for the Independent Confidential Telephone Hotline Service are listed on our corporation intranet. The employee can use the hotline to report the concern initially on a strictly confidential basis. In order to document the details of the alleged wrongdoing to help the audit committee investigate the concern to conclusion, the preferred method is to submit them in writing to any member of the audit committee at the address provided by the Independent Hotline Service, which assures that the complaint will go to an address <u>outside</u> of the corporation and not be seen by anyone within the corporation. Given the sensitivity of such matters, we request that you label the correspondence *"Confidential."*

Employees may submit concerns on a confidential, anonymous basis. If an employee does not want to be identified with the submission, he or she should not include his or her name in the correspondence, but, instead, indicate prominently on the submission that it is a *"Confidential, Anonymous Employee Submission."*

The corporation will not tolerate any form of retaliation against an employee (1) who submits a good faith complaint about the corporation's accounting, internal accounting controls, or auditing practices, or (2) who assists in an investigation of challenged practices.

Director Complaints

Any director who has a concern regarding what he or she views as questionable accounting or auditing practices should bring these concerns to the attention of the audit committee.

A director serving on the audit committee should raise any such concerns at the first audit committee meeting held after he or she becomes concerned.

Other Complaints

Corporation employees and directors should forward to a member of the audit committee any complaint received by them regarding accounting, internal accounting controls, or auditing matters that have not been resolved to the satisfaction of the individual(s) who raised the complaint.

Processing Complaints

The audit committee will schedule a portion of each regularly scheduled audit committee meeting for discussion of recently received complaints. In addition, if a member of the audit committee receives a complaint that in the judgment of such member warrants consideration prior to the next scheduled meeting, that member will attempt to convene a special meeting of the committee to discuss such complaint prior to the next regularly scheduled meeting.

If the audit committee concludes, based on a discussion of a complaint, that such complaint is baseless or frivolous, no further action will be taken, and the audit committee will document the basis for this conclusion.

If the audit committee is not able to conclude at the outset that a complaint is baseless or frivolous, it will conduct an investigation into the complaint. The specific approach to dealing with a particular complaint will depend on facts and circumstances. To the extent the audit committee deems appropriate, the committee also may engage outside advisors to assist in the investigation. (See also chapter 8, "Engaging Independent Counsel and Other Advisers," in this toolkit.) As a general practice, the audit committee, either directly or through advisors, will interview the employees or outside auditors involved in the subject matter of the complaint.

If, following an investigation, the audit committee determines that corrective action is appropriate, the audit committee will, to the extent it has the requisite authority, implement such corrective action on an expeditious basis and, to the extent the audit committee lacks the authority to implement such corrective action, it will recommend a course of action to the full board of directors.

If, following an investigation, the audit committee determines that no corrective action is appropriate, the audit committee will conclude the investigation, noting the basis for its determination.

Retention of Complaints

The chairman of the audit committee, on behalf of the corporation, will enter all complaints in a log (see the "Tracking Report") and maintain a file of materials related to complaints concerning the corporation's accounting or auditing practices. These materials will be retained for a period of five years, or for a longer period if required by law.

Instructions for using this tool: Before using this tool, the audit committee should review any applicable state or local laws and regulations, as well as the appropriate rules promulgated by other relevant regulatory bodies, if any.

Sample Tracking Report

Date Submitted	Tracking Number	Description of Complaint	Submitted By*	Current Status**	Actions Taken	
					Date	Comments

* Submitted By Codes: Employee (E); Customer (C); Vendor (V); Shareholder/Owner (S); Other (O)

** Current Status Codes: R—Resolved; UI—Under Investigation; D—Dismissed; W—Withdrawn; P—Pending/No Action

Chapter 12
Issues Report from Management

Overview: The sample report in this chapter is to be used by management when considering significant issues, estimates, and judgments that may have a material impact on the company's financial statements, among other concerns. Management should be encouraged to use this tool as a means to document any significant issues, judgments, and estimates for discussion with the audit committee. Each matter should be prepared as a separate issues report. Statements should be clear and concise. Some issues may carry over to subsequent meetings, in which case, any updated information should be included in bold.

In many cases, management will communicate with the audit committee regarding the company's accounting policies, practices and estimates; and the audit firm participates in the discussion and confirms that management has adequately communicated the required matters.

Defining Significant Issues, Critical Accounting Estimates, Significant Unusual Transactions, and Judgments

As a first step to any discussion of this nature, it is important for the audit committee to define its threshold for significant issues, critical accounting estimates, significant unusual transactions, and judgments. A significant issue, critical accounting estimates, significant unusual transactions, or judgment is one that

1. creates controversy among members of the management team, or between management and the internal or independent auditors, or where there may be a lack of authoritative guidance or consensus in practice;

2. has or will have a material impact on the financial statements, such as a critical accounting estimate or significant unusual transaction;

3. is or will be a matter of public interest or exposure;

4. must be reported in an upcoming filing with an external body, and management is unclear or undecided on its presentation;

5. applies a new accounting standard. Note that the application of a new accounting standard may or may not be considered a significant issue, estimate, or judgment for the organization. However, for the record, the audit committee may ask management to use this format as a means to brief the audit committee on the application of the new standard;

6. applies to initial selection or changes to significant accounting policies or application of such policies in the current period;

7. relates to the application of a standard in a way that is not consistent with general practice;

8. relates to key controls over financial information that are being designed, redesigned, have failed, or otherwise are being addressed by the organization;

9. is used for consultation with other accountants;

10. uncorrects or corrects misstatements.

The audit committee needs to be proactive and consistent in its inquiries regarding significant issues, estimates, and judgments. At each meeting, the audit committee should inquire about current or unresolved issues or problems that have arisen in the financial, compliance, or operational control environment. Management's response should be documented in the meeting minutes. Management's report to the audit committee concerning significant issues, estimates, and judgments should contain the following elements for a proper basis of discussion by the audit committee:

1. *Definition of the Significant Issue, Estimate, or Judgment.* In this section of the issues report, management should define and summarize the issue as concisely and clearly as possible.

2. *Management's Position.* This section should address management's position on the issue. If there is disagreement among members of management, those disagreements should be identified here as explicitly as possible, with brief explanations of why each member of the management team has taken his or her respective position.

3. *Relevant Literature.* Any professional literature or regulatory requirements addressing this issue should be cited here. If no professional literature is available, it would be appropriate to define industry practice in this space. If this is a developing area, and there is neither accepted industry practice nor other sources to support and refute these positions, this fact should be reported. If there was a choice on the accounting treatment, it should be disclosed here, along with a discussion of how the choices of treatment were compared and the basis on which the final choice was made.

4. *Risks.* Management should identify various risks (both good and bad) associated with this proposal.

5. *Regulatory Disclosure (if applicable).* Management must inform the audit committee about how it intends to address this issue in required filings with regulatory bodies as required by law (for example, insurance commissions, banking authorities, or others).

6. *Auditor's Position.* Has management consulted with the independent auditors on this issue? Do they agree with management's position? Have they addressed the audit issues that might be associated with it? If so, use this section of the issues report to discuss their position. If not, use this section to state explicitly that the auditors have not been consulted.

7. *Other Information Relating to This Issue, Estimate, or Judgment.* Management should use this section of the issues report to highlight other related and relevant information that is not already included in the sections above.

Sample Issues Report From Management

1. *Define the Significant Issue, Estimate, Unusual Transaction, or Judgment.* The company uses the percentage of completion method for revenue recognition on its construction contracts. This year, the company has two large condominium projects in progress that represent 44 percent of revenues and 62 percent of gross profit.

2. *Management's Position.* The procedure and valuations follow the same calculations and assumptions as in previous periods.

3. *Relevant Literature.* FASB ASC 605-35, *Revenue Recognition: Construction-Type and Production-Type Contracts*, FASB ASC 910, *Industry: Contractors-Construction*, and the AICPA Audit and Accounting Guide, Construction Contractors, updated by the AICPA as of May 2012.

4. *Risks.* The profitability of the company is dependent on correct valuation and revenue recognition on these two contracts. If the current assumptions are substantially wrong, then bidding on several upcoming condominium projects would likely be altered.

5. *Regulatory Disclosure.* This issue is not applicable at this point in the discussion, but the bonding agency has requested additional information and the status of current financial statements.

6. *Auditor's Position.* The auditors have not been consulted on this issue yet. However, they did certify the previous year's financial statements, which included the valuation of contracts on the percentage of completion method. At the time, they did not raise any issues about the valuation beyond routine discussions with management.

7. *Other Information Relating to This Issue, Estimate, or Judgment.* One of the project managers has over a dozen years of experience; for the other, this assignment is his second as project manager. Project managers' incentive pay is influenced by timely completion and profitability of projects they manage, and their status reports are the key input on which the controller's office relies to account for in-process projects.

In addition, a new Accounting Standard, *Revenue from Contracts with Customers (Topic 606)*, was issued by FASB in May 2014, and while not yet effective, the company has not yet evaluated the impact this may have on future revenue recognition.

Issues Report From Management

1. *Define the Significant Issue, Estimate, Unusual Transaction, or Judgment.*

2. *Management's Position.*

3. *Relevant Literature.*

4. *Risks.*

5. *SEC Disclosure (or other regulatory disclosure).*

6. *Auditor's Position.*

7. *Other Information Relating to This Issue, Estimate, Unusual Transaction, or Judgment.*

Chapter 13
Guidelines and Questions for Conducting an Audit Committee Executive Session

> **Overview:** It is generally accepted practice that audit committees should hold executive sessions with executive management, leaders of the financial management team, the leader of the internal audit team, and the independent auditor. The "Additional Questions to Consider" tool at the end of this chapter is designed to provide guidance as to the amplitude of the questions that should be asked. It is intended to assist the audit committee in asking the right *first* questions, with the understanding that the audit committee should have the necessary expertise to evaluate the answers and the insight to identify the appropriate follow-up question(s). The tool also contains possible follow-up questions audit committee members can ask key members of the financial management team in order to improve their understanding of the day-to-day operating environment as well as management teams' decision-making processes and interactions.

What Is an Executive Session?

An executive session is a best practice employed by audit committees for any reason. Here, we are advocating that the executive session be used to meet with key members of the executive management and financial management teams on a one-on-one basis. Executive sessions should occur at every meeting of the audit committee, though not every individual need be in an executive session at every meeting. For example, it is appropriate for the chief audit executive (CAE) and the independent auditor to have an executive session at every meeting, but the director of financial reporting might be in executive session with the audit committee only at the meeting before year-end results are released.

During an executive session meeting, minutes are usually not recorded, and when meeting with specific members of the financial management team, anyone who is not a member of the audit committee is excluded from the meeting. The purpose is to ask questions of various members of staff in a safe environment. Executive sessions should be a matter of routine at every audit committee meeting, rather than an exception. In open session, the audit committee should avoid asking whether an individual has anything to discuss in an executive session; that question alone could put the individual in an awkward position with others in the company and deter the purpose of executive sessions. The questions for the executive session are presented in a manner that the discussants may not feel free to answer honestly in the open environment but are designed to promote "safety" within an executive session. In addition, there may be other information that the audit committee wants to know.

Asking open-ended questions in this kind of environment could be a major source of information for the audit committee. This tool includes examples of the types and depth of questions the audit committee should ask. These are meant to be sample questions to help start a conversation and create dialogue between the individual and the audit committee. ***These sample questions are not intended to be a comprehensive checklist.*** Audit committee members must have the expertise not only to understand the answers to the questions, but also to use these answers to develop appropriate follow-up questions. It will not be unusual to ask similar questions of key executives, the independent auditor, or the internal auditor, as a comparison of their respective responses is a good source of insight. Depending on the answers, follow-up action may also be necessary, and the audit committee must be prepared to take that action. The most important thing to do when conducting an executive session is to *listen to the answers that are given and follow up on anything that you do not understand*!

Audit committee members should also consider the history of the company, the industry in which it operates, the current economic climate, the competitive environment, and other factors when asking questions in executive session. Finally, the audit committee should remind the member of management that its members are accessible even outside the meeting, and that he or she should feel free to contact the audit committee members at other times if the need arises.

It is important to note that not every organization will have different individuals in each position, as assumed in the following questions. Nevertheless, the audit committee should be aware of the functions that are part of dual roles, and adjust the questions accordingly. For example, in a small company, the CFO and controller might share the duties of the director of financial reporting. The audit committee should explore how a function or role is accomplished, and compose questions appropriately. Also, the audit committee should consider and take into account other roles in the organization. It may be that other people within an organization should be asked to meet with the audit committee in executive session.

Additional Questions to Consider: Tool for Audit Committee Members

Purpose of this tool: As a part of fulfilling your responsibilities as an audit committee member, this tool is intended to help you consider the types of questions you should be asking management during audit committee meetings or executive sessions. Your audit committee should be made up of members who have the expertise to evaluate the answers and the insight to identify the appropriate follow-up question. Also, the performance evaluations section has additional evaluation questions concerning the performance of the internal audit team, independent auditor, and audit committee.

Note: There are four categories of questions (Fraud/Ethics, Internal Environment, Independent Auditor, Financial Statements) and eight positions of whom you might ask the same question (CEO, CFO, CAE, general counsel, controller, CIO, and independent auditor).

Sample Questions to Ask During Audit Committee Meetings/Executive Sessions

Question	Concept	Position							Comments
		CEO	CFO	CAE	General Counsel	Controller	CIO	Independent Auditor	
1. Do you believe the financial statements present the company's financial position fairly?	Financial Statements	X	X	X		X		X	
2. Has the company solicited or received advice from or given advice to any outside party on how to structure any transaction to produce a desired financial statement effect? If so, please provide details.	Financial Statements		X	X	X	X			
3. Do you believe the disclosures are adequate and that the average user of the financial statements will understand them?	Financial Statements	X	X	X		X			
4. Are you satisfied that an appropriate audit was performed by the independent auditors?	Independent Auditor	X	X	X		X	X		
5. Are you aware of any situations of earnings management in the company?	Fraud/Ethics	X	X	X	X	X			

Sample Questions to Ask During Audit Committee Meetings/Executive Sessions

Question	Concept	CEO	CFO	CAE	General Counsel	Controller	CIO	Independent Auditor	Comments
6. Are you aware of any current or past fraud occurrence or any kind of fraud in the organization? Do you know of any situations in which fraud could occur?	Fraud/Ethics	X	X	X	X	X	X	X	
7. Have you encountered any situations in which the organization complied with legal minimums of behavior, yet failed to go the extra mile to demonstrate its commitment to the highest ethical standards?	Fraud/Ethics	X	X	X	X	X	X	X	
8. Do you feel comfortable raising issues without fear of retribution?	Fraud/Ethics		X	X	X	X	X	X	
9. Are you aware of any disagreements between the company's management team and the independent auditors?	Independent Auditor	X	X	X	X	X	X	X	
10. Are you aware of any disagreements between the company's management team and the internal auditors?	Internal Environment	X	X	X	X	X	X	X	

(continued)

Sample Questions to Ask During Audit Committee Meetings/Executive Sessions

Question	Concept	Position							Comments
		CEO	CFO	CAE	General Counsel	Controller	CIO	Independent Auditor	
11. Is there any activity at the executive level of management that you consider to be a violation of laws, regulations, GAAP, professional practice, or the mores of business?	Fraud/Ethics	X	X	X	X	X	X	X	
12. Are there any questions we have not asked that we should have asked? If so, what are those questions?	Misc.	X	X	X	X	X	X	X	
13. Overall, is management cooperating with the internal audit team? Does management have a positive attitude in responding to findings and recommendations, or is it insecure and defensive of findings?	Internal Environment	X	X	X	X	X	X	X	
14. Has management set an appropriate tone at the top with respect to the importance of and compliance with the internal control system around financial reporting?	Internal Environment			X		X	X	X	

Sample Questions to Ask During Audit Committee Meetings/Executive Sessions

Question	Concept	Position							Comments
		CEO	CFO	CAE	General Counsel	Controller	CIO	Independent Auditor	
15. Discuss areas in which there is an accounting treatment that could be construed as aggressive. Has the organization taken any tax positions that could be construed as aggressive?	Financial Statements	X	X	X		X		X	
16. Do you have the freedom to conduct audits as necessary throughout the company?	Internal Environment			X					
17. Were you restricted or denied access to requested information?	Internal Environment			X					
18. Have you been pressured to change findings, or minimize the language in those findings so as to not reflect badly on another member of management? Are findings and recommendations given the level of discussion needed to satisfy any issues raised to your satisfaction?	Fraud/Ethics			X					
19. If you were the CFO, how would you change the financial statements and accompanying footnotes?	Financial Statements					X			

(continued)

Sample Questions to Ask During Audit Committee Meetings/Executive Sessions

Question	Concept	Position							Comments
		CEO	CFO	CAE	General Counsel	Controller	CIO	Independent Auditor	
20. Are you aware of any disagreements between the company's management and the independent auditors?	Independent Auditor					X			
21. Are there any issues since our last meeting that you wish to discuss with the audit committee?	Misc.	X	X	X	X	X	X	X	
22. Do you believe the financial statements and related disclosures convey the company's financial situation adequately to an average investor?	Financial Statements		X			X			
23. Now that you have the opportunity, is there anything you want to tell the audit committee? Is there anything else that we need to know?	Misc.	X	X	X	X	X	X		
24. Are you satisfied with the presentation of information about the company in the 10-K, 10-Qs, proxy statements, and other filings?	Financial Statements				X				

Sample Questions to Ask During Audit Committee Meetings/Executive Sessions

Question	Concept	Position							Comments
		CEO	CFO	CAE	General Counsel	Controller	CIO	Independent Auditor	
25. Are you aware of any issues that could cause embarrassment to the company?	Internal Environment				X				
26. Have you ever been told anything in confidence or otherwise that would embarrass the company if it were known publicly?	Internal Environment				X				
27. Are there any items that you have discussed with the CEO, CFO, other officers, or outside counsel of which the audit committee is not already aware?	Internal Environment				X				
28. Is there any activity in the organization with which you are uncomfortable, consider unusual, or that you believe warrants further investigation?	Internal Environment		X	X	X	X	X	X	

(continued)

Sample Questions to Ask During Audit Committee Meetings/Executive Sessions

Question	Concept	Position							Comments
		CEO	CFO	CAE	General Counsel	Controller	CIO	Independent Auditor	
29. Explain the process your firm uses to assure that all of your engagement personnel are independent and objective with respect to our audit. Particularly, with respect to nonaudit services, how do those services affect the work that you do or the manner in which the engagement team or others are compensated? Are you aware of any anticipated event that could possibly impair the independence, in fact or in appearance, of the firm or any member of the engagement team?	Independent Auditor							X	
30. Have management, legal counsel, or others made you aware of anything that could be considered a violation of laws, regulations, GAAP, professional practice, or the ethics of business?	Independent Auditor							X	

Sample Questions to Ask During Audit Committee Meetings/Executive Sessions

Question	Concept	Position								Comments
		CEO	CFO	CAE	General Counsel	Controller	CIO	Independent Auditor	
31. Are there any areas of the financial statements, including the notes, in which you believe we could be more explicit or transparent, or provide more clarity to help a user understand our financial statements more fully?	Independent Auditor							X	
32. Have you expressed any concerns or offered comments to management with respect to how our presentation, including the notes or Management's Discussion and Analysis could be improved?	Independent Auditor							X	
33. Which accounting policies or significant business transactions do you think an investor will have trouble understanding based on our disclosure? What additional information should we provide?	Independent Auditor							X	

(continued)

Sample Questions to Ask During Audit Committee Meetings/Executive Sessions

Question	Concept	Position							Comments
		CEO	CFO	CAE	General Counsel	Controller	CIO	Independent Auditor	
34. Based on your auditing procedures, do you have any concerns that management may be attempting to manage earnings, either properly or improperly? Have you noticed any biases as a result of your audit tests with respect to estimates?	Independent Auditor							X	
35. In which areas have you and management disagreed?	Independent Auditor							X	
36. Discuss your impressions of the performance of the CAE in terms of the completeness, accuracy, and faithfulness of the financial reporting process.	Independent Auditor							X	
37. Has the firm been engaged to provide any services besides the independent audit of which the audit committee is not already aware?	Independent Auditor							X	
38. How can management improve in terms of setting an appropriate tone at the top?	Independent Auditor							X	

Sample Questions to Ask During Audit Committee Meetings/Executive Sessions

Question	Concept	Position								Comments
		CEO	CFO	CAE	General Counsel	Controller	CIO	Independent Auditor	
39. Describe the ideas you have discussed with management for improving the financial reporting internal control system.	Independent Auditor							X	
40. Describe any situation in which you believe management has attempted to circumvent the spirit of GAAP, though it has complied with GAAP.	Independent Auditor							X	
41. Is there anything going on in the organization with which you are uncomfortable, that you consider unusual, or that warrants further investigation?	Independent Auditor							X	
42. Are there any questions we have not asked that you wish to discuss with the audit committee?	Independent Auditor							X	
43. Describe your working relationship with the CEO.	Internal Environment		X						
44. If you were the partner-in-charge of the audit, what would you do differently?	Internal Environment		X			X			

(continued)

Sample Questions to Ask During Audit Committee Meetings/Executive Sessions

Question	Concept	Position								Comments
		CEO	CFO	CAE	General Counsel	Controller	CIO	Independent Auditor	
45. How do you interface with the internal audit function, and do you believe it is successful?	Internal Environment		X						
46. Has the independent auditor been engaged for any services other than the annual audit of which the audit committee is not already aware?	Independent Auditor	X	X	X	X	X			
47. What issues arose from any internal control documentation and validation efforts?	Internal Environment	X	X						
48. What aspects of the business put the most strain on company liquidity? On the company's capital position?	Financial Statements		X						
49. Which systems are the most difficult to use?	Internal Environment		X						
50. Are there any new systems or functionality that you would like to purchase but have delayed due to cost considerations?	Internal Environment		X						

Sample Questions to Ask During Audit Committee Meetings/Executive Sessions

Question	Concept	Position								Comments
		CEO	CFO	CAE	General Counsel	Controller	CIO	Independent Auditor		
51. What procedures or oversight do you apply to manual journal entries that are proposed during the book-closing process?	Financial Statements		X							
52. Do the accounting and finance departments of the company have adequate personnel, both in numbers and quality, to meet all their obligations?	Internal Environment		X							
53. What are the most difficult challenges facing the finance organization today?	Internal Environment		X							
54. Which departments might benefit the most from additional personnel?	Internal Environment		X							
55. What were the personnel turnover rates in the accounting and finance teams for the last year?	Internal Environment		X							

(continued)

Sample Questions to Ask During Audit Committee Meetings/Executive Sessions

| Question | Concept | Position | | | | | | | Comments |
		CEO	CFO	CAE	General Counsel	Controller	CIO	Independent Auditor	
56. Which of the company's lines of business and operations had the biggest negative impact on earnings this past year? The biggest positive impact? What, if any, changes do you believe need to be made in these areas?	Financial Statements	X	X	X		X		X	
57. Describe your working relationship with the heads of the respective business units.	Internal Environment	X	X	X	X		X		
58. What are the biggest risks facing the company in the next year? What steps do you think the company should take to address those risks?	Internal Environment	X	X	X	X	X	X	X	
59. What are the biggest risks facing the company over the long term? What measures do you believe the company should take to address those risks?	Internal Environment	X	X	X	X	X	X	X	

Sample Questions to Ask During Audit Committee Meetings/Executive Sessions

Question	Concept	Position								Comments
		CEO	CFO	CAE	General Counsel	Controller	CIO	Independent Auditor	
60. In light of the fact that you certified to your review of the financial statements that the financial statements do not contain any untrue statement of material fact or omit material facts, that they present fairly the results of operations, and that you take responsibility for the design of the internal control system, and have evaluated the effectiveness of the internal control system, what were your areas of concern? Are you satisfied that those areas have been resolved?	Financial Statements	X	X						
61. What procedures do you apply to the review of manual journal entries made during the book-closing process, and to other entries that could be termed as a management override of the internal control system around financial reporting?	Financial Statements			X		X			

(continued)

		Concept	Position								Comments
			CEO	CFO	CAE	General Counsel	Controller	CIO	Independent Auditor		
Question											
62.	If you were the CEO, how would you do things differently in the internal audit department?	Internal Environment			X						
63.	Do you believe you have adequate resources available to you to fulfill the charge of the department? If not, what additional resources are needed?	Internal Environment			X						
64.	Did you encounter any disagreements or difficulties between the internal audit team and the independent auditors in connection with the recently completed audit of the company's financial statements? How will you approach the financial statement audit differently next year?	Internal Environment			X						

Sample Questions to Ask During Audit Committee Meetings/Executive Sessions

Sample Questions to Ask During Audit Committee Meetings/Executive Sessions

Question	Concept	Position							Comments
		CEO	CFO	CAE	General Counsel	Controller	CIO	Independent Auditor	
65. What critical risks are being monitored by the internal audit team on a periodic or regular basis? How do you address the continuous auditing of these critical risks, and are automation and integrated system reporting assisting you in this effort?	Internal Environment			X					
66. Are you aware of any other disagreements between the company's management and the independent auditors?	Internal Environment	X	X	X	X	X	X		
67. Are there any disagreements between the internal audit team and management?	Internal Environment	X	X	X	X	X	X	X	
68. What issues arose from any control documentation and validation efforts?	Financial Statements	X	X	X		X	X	X	
69. Are the computer systems upon which you rely integrated, or is manual intervention required to integrate your systems?	Internal Environment		X			X	X		
70. What is your assessment of the CAE's performance?	Internal Environment	X	X		X	X	X	X	

(continued)

Sample Questions to Ask During Audit Committee Meetings/Executive Sessions

Question	Concept	Position							Comments
		CEO	CFO	CAE	General Counsel	Controller	CIO	Independent Auditor	
71. Have you been asked to provide assurance to the CFO and CEO about your role in the financial reporting process? Is the requested assurance similar to the certifications that the CEO and CFO must make to regulatory bodies?	Financial Statements	X				X			
72. How could the financial statements and related disclosures be improved?	Financial Statements	X	X	X		X		X	
73. Are you satisfied with the integrity of the information running through the systems in the company? How could technology improve the integrity of the information?	Internal Environment	X	X	X		X	X		
74. From what exposure does the company's firewall protect the company's sensitive data?	Internal Environment	X		X			X	X	
75. If you had an unlimited budget, how would you spend money to improve the company's information architecture?	Internal Environment						X		

Sample Questions to Ask During Audit Committee Meetings/Executive Sessions

Question	Concept	Position							Comments
		CEO	CFO	CAE	General Counsel	Controller	CIO	Independent Auditor	
76. What do you consider your critical risk areas?	Internal Environment	X	X	X	X	X	X		
77. Describe your relationship with the CEO, CFO, and other key people in the accounting and finance teams.	Internal Environment			X	X	X	X		
78. Are manual journal entries identified and approved? Are they somehow brought to the attention of the CAE or other officers who did not have a hand in creating the journal entries?	Financial Statements		X	X		X		X	
79. Is documentation updated every time there is a change to the internal controls process?	Internal Environment		X	X		X	X		
80. What role, if any, did your firm have in management's documentation and assessment of the company's internal control structure?	Independent Auditor							X	

(continued)

Sample Questions to Ask During Audit Committee Meetings/Executive Sessions

Question	Concept	Position								Comments
		CEO	CFO	CAE	General Counsel	Controller	CIO	Independent Auditor	
81. What audit procedures do you apply to manual journal entries that are proposed during the book-closing process, or to other journal entries that could be termed as management overrides of the internal control system around financial reporting?	Independent Auditor							X	
82. Was any audit work not performed due to any limitations placed on you by management, such as any areas scoped out by management, or any restriction on fees that limited the scope of your work?	Independent Auditor							X	
83. Was the audit fee that you charged the company sufficient for the work that you performed?	Independent Auditor							X	
84. If you had had an unlimited audit fee, what additional work would you have performed?	Independent Auditor							X	

Chapter 14

Independent Auditor Communications with Audit Committee

> **Overview:** The audit committee's responsibility to oversee the company's financial reporting and disclosures is increasingly challenging as the requirements and complexity of accounting standards continue to grow. This chapter is designed to help the audit committee fulfill its responsibilities with respect to oversight of the company's accounting and financial reporting, as well as oversight of the independent audit firm, by addressing key required communications between independent auditors and audit committees. Clear communication among the audit committee, management, and the independent auditor (auditor) are essential to the effective discharge of these responsibilities. The required communications are based on AICPA auditing standards and are intended to enhance the relevance, timeliness, and quality of communications between the auditor and the audit committee, and to foster constructive dialogue and enhanced understanding about significant audit and financial statement matters. While the communications addressed in this tool are described as those between the auditor and the audit committee, part or all of the communication could be with the chair of the audit committee, the full board of directors, or others in the company that the auditor finds meeting the description of "those charged with governance."

Background

The Sarbanes Oxley Act of 2002 (the Act) contained a number of reforms intended to improve the integrity of accounting and financial disclosure. Although the Act applies to public companies, it led to changes in auditing standards for required communications between the auditor and the audit committee (or those charged with corporate governance) related to all financial statement audits. When those charged with governance are also involved in managing the company, as is often the case with smaller entities, the auditor must consider whether communication with management, and especially management with financial reporting responsibilities, adequately informs those charged with governance. Therefore, the audit committee must ensure they have reached an understanding with the auditor of appropriate levels of communication under those circumstances. Items noted herein as PCAOB or SEC requirements may be considered best practice although not required for private companies.

Objectives of Communications

The following sections summarize matters that may be communicated and are not meant to describe all topics that the auditor is communicating to the audit committee, only the minimum required communication. Broadly speaking, the required communications[1] cover the following four objectives and other significant communications for the auditor's communications with the audit committee:

---

[1] AU-C sec. 260, *The Auditor's Communication With Those Charged With Governance* (AICPA, *Professional Standards*).

- Communicate the auditor's responsibilities and establish terms of the firm's audit engagement
- Inquire of the audit committee about matters relevant to the audit
- Communicate audit strategy, scope, timing, and approach, including accounting policies, practices and estimates
- Provide timely observations that are significant to the financial reporting process, including the audit firm's evaluation of the quality of the company's financial reporting

Timing of Communications

Audit committee communications should be made in a timely manner and prior to the issuance of the auditor's report. The appropriate timing of a particular communication to the audit committee depends on factors such as the significance of the matters to be communicated and corrective or follow-up action needed. Communications may be made to only the audit committee chair if doing so helps with timeliness; however, all such matters should be communicated to the audit committee prior to the issuance of the auditor's report. Although this section focuses primarily on communications by the auditor, communications among management, the auditor, and the audit committee are important in assisting the committee fulfill its responsibility to oversee the financial statement process and other matters of governance interest. Communications by the auditor do not relieve management of this responsibility.

1. Terms of the Firm's Audit Engagement

Terms of the audit and engagement letter. The audit firm must establish an understanding of the terms of the engagement with the audit committee, and, in an engagement letter must include the objectives of the audit, the responsibilities of the auditor, and the responsibilities of management. It is important for the audit committee to understand what an audit is and what it is not, and the auditor's engagement terms should clearly describe the auditor's responsibilities under general accepted auditing standards.

Discussions with management in connection with appointment or retention. The auditors must discuss with the audit committee any significant issues that the audit firm discussed with management in connection with the audit firm's appointment or retention, including any significant discussions regarding the application of accounting principles and auditing standards. Although under SOX the audit committee has responsibility for appointment or retention of the audit firm, the rule acknowledges that it may rely on management in making its decision.

Independence. Generally accepted auditing standards require independence for all audits. Although the auditor's report affirms the auditor's independence, the auditor should communicate to the audit committee circumstances such as financial interests, business or family relationships, or nonaudit services provided that, in the auditor's judgment, may be thought to bear on independence and that the auditor considered in reaching the conclusion that independence has not been impaired.

2. Inquiries About Matters Relevant to the Audit

The audit firm must ask the audit committee whether it is aware of matters relevant to the audit including, but not limited to, violations or possible violations of laws or regulations or risks of material misstatement, including inquiries related to fraud risk. Although not required, an audit firm may choose to seek a representation letter from the audit committee addressing such matters.

The auditor may also discuss with the audit committee his or her view about roles and responsibilities between those charged with governance and management, how those charged with governance oversee the effectiveness of internal control and the detection or possibility of fraud, significant communications with regulators, or other matters deemed relevant to the audit of the financial statements.

Auditing Standard No. 12 (AS 12), *Identifying and Assessing Risks of Material Misstatement*, requires the audit firm to make specific inquiries of the audit committee, management, internal audit, and others within the company regarding their views of fraud risks within the company. The specific required inquiries of the audit committee include the committee's views about fraud risks in the company; whether the audit committee has knowledge of fraud, alleged fraud, or suspected fraud affecting the company; whether the audit committee is aware of tips or complaints regarding the company's financial reporting (including those received through the internal whistleblower program, if such a program exists), and if so, the audit committee's responses to such tips and complaints; and how the audit committee exercises oversight of the company's assessment of fraud risks and the establishment of controls to address fraud risks.

3. Audit Strategy, Timing, and Approach

Communicating the Audit Strategy and Timing. As part of communicating overall audit strategy, the auditor must specifically communicate the timing of the audit, discuss significant risks identified during risk assessment procedures, and, if applicable, discuss the following:

- The nature and extent of specialized skills or knowledge required to perform procedures or evaluate results related to significant risks
- The approach for internal control relevant to the audit including, when applicable, whether the auditor will express an opinion on the effectiveness of internal control over financial report
- If applicable, the extent to which the firm will rely on company internal auditors or other parties in connection with the audit
- The names and responsibilities of others not employed by the audit firm who perform audit procedures
- The basis for the auditor's determination that it can serve as the principal auditor, if significant parts of the audit are performed by other auditors
- The concept of materiality in planning and executing the audit
- Confirmation of the appropriate person or people in the entity's governance structure with whom to communicate

Critical Accounting Policies and Practices. The auditor must inform the audit committee of all critical accounting policies and how they are applied in the company. Critical accounting policies are those that are both most important to the portrayal of the company's financial condition and require management's most difficult, subjective or complex judgments, often as a result of the need to make estimates about the effects of matters that are inherently uncertain. The audit committee should expect the following communications:

- All critical accounting policies, including those that applied for the first time during the year, changes in accounting policies, or accounting practices that are not specifically addressed in the accounting literature, for example, those that may be unique to a specific industry
- The reason certain policies and practices are considered critical
- How those accounting policies are applied in the organization
- Policies and practices the organization used to account for significant unusual transactions
- The effect on the financial statements or disclosures of critical accounting policies in controversial or emerging areas for which there is lack of authoritative guidance or consensus, or diversity in practice, such as revenue recognition, off-balance-sheet financing, or accounting for equity investments
- Whether these critical policies are included in the financial statements

Critical Accounting Estimates. Critical accounting estimates are an integral part of the financial statements prepared by management. These estimates are based on management's judgments (which are normally based on management's knowledge and experience about past and current events), and assumptions about future events.

The auditor should address the following issues with the audit committee:

a. The process used by management to develop critical accounting estimates
b. Management's significant assumptions in developing critical accounting estimates that have a high degree of subjectivity
c. For any significant changes to (a) or (b), a description of management's reasons for the changes and the effects of the changes on the financial statements
d. The basis for the auditor's conclusion about the reasonableness of those estimates

In many cases, management will communicate with the audit committee regarding the company's accounting policies, practices, and estimates. The audit firm participates in the discussion and confirms that management has communicated the required matters adequately.

4. Evaluation of the Quality of the Company's Financial Reporting

The auditor must communicate judgments about the quality, not only factual information and conclusions regarding the acceptability of the organization's accounting policies and practices. The communication should be tailored to the organization's specific circumstances and include evaluation of the following:

- **Significant Accounting Policies and Practices:** Auditor's conclusions about the qualitative aspects, including the auditor's assessment of management's disclosures. Communication must include any situation in which the auditor identified bias in management's judgments about the amounts or disclosures, and evaluation of differences between estimates supported by audit evidence and estimates included in the financial statements.

- **Critical Accounting Estimates:** The basis for auditor's conclusions regarding estimates, judgments and uncertainties underlying financial statements and conclusions.

- **Significant Unusual Transactions:** The auditor's understanding of the business rationale for significant unusual transactions.

- **Financial Statement Presentation:** Evaluation of whether presentation of financial statements and disclosures are in conformity with the applicable financial reporting framework.

- **New Accounting Pronouncements:** If applicable, any concern regarding significant effects on future financial reporting related to management's anticipated application of accounting pronouncements that have been issued but are not yet effective.

- **Alternative Accounting Treatments:** Permissible alternative accounting treatments related to material items, ramifications thereof, and the treatment preferred by the auditor.

5. Other Significant Communications

In addition to communications about the quality of financial reporting noted in Section 4, the auditor must communicate, when relevant, the following regarding the audit process and results.

Responsibility for Other Information. Although the notes to the financial statements are an integral part of the financial statements and therefore are included in the scope of the auditing procedures, other information prepared by management that may accompany financial statements is not necessarily included in the scope of the auditing procedures. The auditor should communicate his or her responsibility for such information, and the results of any relate procedures performed.

Matters for Which the Auditor Consulted. The auditor should communicate any difficult or contentious matters for which the auditor consulted outside the engagement team, which may include the firm's national office, industry specialists, or an external party.

Matters for Which Management Consulted. Sometimes, management of the company may consult with other independent accountants about significant accounting or auditing matters. If the auditor is aware that such consultation has occurred, the auditor should discuss with the audit committee their views about the significant matters that were the subject of the consultation.

Material Written Communications. The auditor should notify the audit committee of other material communications with management, such as the management letter, schedule of unadjusted differences, and written representations the auditor is requesting from management.

Uncorrected and Corrected Misstatements. The auditor should inform the audit committee about all corrected and uncorrected misstatements arising from the audit that could, in the auditor's judgment, have a significant effect on the entity's financial reporting process. The audit engagement team tracks proposed adjustments during the audit, except for those that are clearly trivial, for discussion with management. Management evaluates those proposed adjustments and determines whether or not to record the adjustments.

The auditor's communications should

- inform the audit committee about adjustments arising from the audit that could have a significant effect, either individually or in the aggregate, on the organization's financial reporting process;
- address whether or not the proposed adjustments were recorded, and the implications of any misstatements on the company's financial reporting process;
- address whether the adjustments to accounts and disclosures may not have been detected except through the auditing procedures performed (meaning that the organization's own internal control system did not detect the need for the adjustment); and
- provide the schedule of uncorrected misstatements related to both accounts and disclosures, and support for the determination that the uncorrected adjustments were immaterial, including qualitative factors.

Departure from the Auditor's Standard Report. The following matters related to modifications of the auditor's standard report should be communicated:

- The reasons for the modification and the wording of the report, if the auditor expects to modify the opinion in the auditor's report
- The reason for and the wording of the explanatory language if the auditor expects to include explanatory language or an explanatory paragraph in the auditor's report

Disagreements With Management. Disagreements may arise between the auditor and management over the application of accounting principles to specific transactions and events, as well as the basis for management's judgments about accounting estimates, or the scope of the audit or disclosures to be made in the financial statements or footnotes. Differences of opinion based on incomplete facts or preliminary information that are later resolved are not considered disagreements for this purpose.

The auditors should communicate any disagreements with management, whether or not satisfactorily resolved, about matters that could be significant, individually or in the aggregate, to the company's financial statements or the auditor's report.

Difficulties Encountered in Performing the Audit. The auditor should inform the audit committee about any significant difficulties encountered in working with management and staff during the audit. Examples include, but are not limited to, an unreasonably brief time to complete the audit, delays or unavailability of needed personnel or information, or unexpected extensive effort required by the auditor to obtain sufficient audit evidence. These difficulties could represent a scope limitation that may result in a modified auditor's opinion, or the auditor's withdrawal from the engagement.

Going Concern. The auditor must communicate those conditions and events the audit firm has identified that, when considered in the aggregate, lead the auditor to believe that there is substantial doubt about the company's ability to continue as a going concern for a reasonable period of time, along with the basis for the conclusion. The auditor must also communicate the effects on the financial statements and on the auditor's report.

Other Matters. Any other matters arising from the audit that are significant to the oversight of the company's financial reporting process should be communicated, including any complaints or concerns regarding accounting or auditing matters that have been conveyed to the audit firm.

Interim Reviews. The audit committee should expect communications from the auditor related to interim reviews to include

- an engagement letter communicating the terms of the engagement to review interim financial information.
- material weaknesses or significant deficiencies, if any, of which the auditor becomes aware.
- other significant matters impacting the interim financial information.
- a schedule of uncorrected misstatements, if any.

Illegal Acts

The auditor has the responsibility to assure himself or herself that the audit committee is adequately informed about illegal acts that come to the auditor's attention (this communication need not include matters that are clearly inconsequential). The communication should describe (1) the act, (2) the circumstances of its occurrence, and (3) the effect on the financial statements.

What is an illegal act for purposes of this communication? Statement on Auditing Standards (SAS) No. 54, *Illegal Acts by Clients* (AICPA, *Professional Standards*, vol. 1, AU sec. 317), defines it as "violations of laws or government regulations attributable to the entity, or acts by management or employees on behalf of the entity. Illegal acts do not include personal misconduct by the entity's personnel unrelated to their business activities."

Internal Control Matters

See also chapter 9, "Internal Control: Guidelines and Tool for the Audit Committee," in this toolkit, which defines key terms used in the assessment of internal controls.

The auditor may communicate in writing to management and the audit committee all significant deficiencies and material weaknesses observed relating to the organization's internal control in the conduct of a financial statement audit. These matters should be discussed with the audit committee because they represent significant deficiencies in the design or operation of the internal control system, which could adversely affect the organization's ability to initiate, record, process, and report financial data consistent with the assertions of management in the financial statements.

The auditor must also communicate to management, in writing or orally, control deficiencies that are not significant. These may be communicated with other observations that may be of potential operational or administrative benefit, including recommendations for improving internal control. This is typically provided in the form of a management letter, or may be combined with required communications noted in the previous paragraph.

Management may be required by a regulator to prepare a written response to the auditor's communication regarding significant deficiencies or material weaknesses identified during the audit. These responses may include a description of corrective action to be taken, plans to implement new controls, or a statement indicating that management believes the cost of correcting the deficiency would exceed the benefits to be derived from doing so.

Fraud

See also chapter 10, "Fraud and the Responsibilities of the Audit Committee: An Overview," in this toolkit.

SAS No. 99, *Consideration of Fraud in a Financial Statement Audit* (AICPA, *Professional Standards*, vol. 1, AU sec. 316), requires that the independent auditor bring any evidence of fraud to the attention of the appropriate level of management (generally seen as one level higher than the level at which a suspected fraud may have occurred), even in the case of an inconsequential fraud, such as a minor defalcation by a low-level employee. The independent auditor should reach an understanding with the audit committee regarding nature and scope when an inconsequential fraud committed by a low-level employee should be brought to the audit committee's attention.

Fraud involving senior management, and any fraud, whether caused by senior management or other employees, that causes a material misstatement of the financial statements must be reported to the audit committee by the independent auditor.

Chapter 15

Responding to the Identification of a Material Weakness— A Checklist for the Audit Committee

Overview: The tool in this chapter is designed to educate the audit committee of a company that has received an adverse report on the effectiveness of its internal control over financial reporting from its independent auditors. The first half of the chapter summarizes the internal control evaluation requirements; the second half includes steps the audit committee should take if faced with this situation. See also chapter 9, "Internal Control: Guidelines and Tool for the Audit Committee," in this toolkit for a more comprehensive discussion of the audit committee's oversight role with respect to internal control.

Background

For public companies, the Sarbanes-Oxley Act of 2002 (the Act) includes a requirement for management to (1) state its responsibility for establishing and maintaining an adequate internal control system over financial reporting, and (2) make an assessment, as of the end of the most recent fiscal year, of the effectiveness of the internal control system over financial reporting. While private companies are not subject to the Act, those charged with corporate governance in all companies should ensure that management maintains and monitors the adequacy of the company's systems of internal control, and should also ensure that management has plans in place to correct identified weaknesses in internal control. Implementing practices that are consistent with the Act is considered best practice and would strengthen corporate governance around financial reporting and related controls. In addition, private companies that plan to become public companies should consider adopting requirements of the Act.

Internal Control Evaluation Requirements

The auditor is required to obtain an understanding of internal control relevant to the audit when identifying and assessing the risks of material misstatement. In making those risk assessments, the auditor considers internal control in order to design audit procedures that are appropriate in the circumstances but not for the purpose of expressing an opinion on the effectiveness of internal control. The auditor may identify deficiencies in internal control not only during this risk assessment process but also at any other stage of the audit.

The auditor may have an additional engagement to report on the effectiveness of an entity's internal control over financial reporting under AT section 501, *An Examination of an Entity's Internal Control Over Financial Reporting That Is Integrated With an Audit of Its Financial Statements* (AICPA, *Professional Standards*). This section does not address an AT section 501 engagement.

To understand control deficiencies best, it is important for audit committee members to understand certain key terms. Review the section "Key Terms in Internal Control Over Financial Reporting Control" in chapter 9, "Internal Control: Guidelines and Tool for the Audit Committee," in this toolkit for definitions and explanations of the terms *control deficiency*, *significant deficiency*, and *material weakness*.

Responding to the Identification of a Material Weakness

Whether a material weakness is identified by management, internal audit, or the auditor, management should have a plan in place to correct the weakness(es), and the audit committee should be engaged in the review and approval of that plan. The checklist in this section provides guidance and questions which the audit committee can ask as part of its review.

Additional Resources

Private companies that are not subject to PCAOB and SEC requirements may want to refer to public company requirements as a resource. The following are various forms of guidance applicable to public companies that may be beneficial to audit committees and management:

- PCAOB Auditing Standard No. 5, *An Audit of Internal Control Over Financial Reporting That Is Integrated with An Audit of Financial Statements*
- PCAOB Auditing Standard No. 4, *Reporting on Whether a Previously Reported Material Weakness Continues to Exist*—guidance related to reporting on a previously identified material weakness that continues to exist
- Frequently asked questions on Management's Report on Internal Control Over Financial Reporting and Certification of Disclosure in Exchange Act Periodic Reports (www.sec.gov/info/accountants/controlfaq.htm)
- Guidance for small businesses regarding their obligations under Section 404 (www.sec.gov/info/smallbus/404guide.shtml)
- SEC Staff Statement on Management's Report on Internal Control Over Financial Reporting (www.sec.gov/info/accountants/stafficreporting.pdf, issued May 16, 2005).
- Commission Guidance Regarding Management's Report on Internal Control Over Financial Reporting Under Section 13(a) or 15(d) of the Securities Exchange Act of 1934 (issued June 27, 2007).

Steps the Audit Committee Can Consider If Faced With an Adverse Report on Internal Control

Instructions for using this tool: In a company facing a negative report on internal control, those charged with governance should take steps to ensure that (1) any material weakness(es) in internal control are swiftly corrected, and (2) key stakeholders are assured that corrective action has been taken.

Note: This tool has been prepared purposefully for broad application. No single tool of a practical length could be developed to address all different situations that could cause a negative report on an organization's internal controls over financial reporting. When faced with a negative report, those charged with governance should use this tool in the context of the deficiencies noted. As with all tools of this type, users must apply their own insight and judgment to the situation to maximize benefits.

It is important for those charged with governance to understand the material weakness(es) giving rise to the negative report. They should meet with the management team, internal auditors, and independent auditors, and understand the issue from each perspective to make fully informed recommendations and decisions. The following are sample questions to help guide the audit committee through this process.

Sample Questions	Comments
Management Team	
1. Interview members of the management team, including the chief financial officer (CFO), controller, and other management, as necessary, closer to the situation, about the weakness(es). You should consider conducting these interviews in an executive session.	
• Who identified the weakness, and in what context, such as routine internal audit or management review was it identified?	
a. Management	
b. Internal audit	
c. Independent auditors	
d. Another third party	
• What are the nature and root cause of the control failure?	
• How long has the weakness existed?	

(continued)

Sample Questions	Comments
Management Team	
• What are the financial statement implications of the control failure? Are there regulatory or compliance implications? Are there reputational implications? Could the control failure have been the result of fraud?	
• If the root cause is systemic, such as turnover, were other controls affected? Are there other controls in the area that may mitigate for the control that failed?	
• What is management's plan and timing to correct the material weakness?	
2. Explore with the management team how much was known about the weakness(es) when the CEO and CFO prepared the financial statements and made certifications regarding those financial statements (if applicable).	
• Consider any implications to these financial statements in light of the material weaknesses noted.	
Those Charged with Governance	
1. Discuss the material weakness with those charged with governance.	
• Are you comfortable with management's assertions about the material weakness and the corrective action plan? Determine whether internal audit, management, or a third party conducted any recent testing in the area and understand the results of their testing.	
• Do you have concerns that fraud or an illegal act was involved in the material weakness?	
• Has management been responsive to findings and recommendations in the past? Has management been cooperative and open during the review of the material weakness?	

Sample Questions	Comments
Independent Auditor	
1. In executive session, discuss the findings, implications, and recommendations with the independent auditor.	
• Determine whether the independent auditor's result is consistent with the result of management's assessment of internal controls.	
2. Collect information from the independent auditor based on his or her knowledge of internal controls and experiences with other clients:	
• Has the weakness been discussed with the company in the past? Does management have proper tone at the top regarding internal controls?	
• Is this weakness a result of a unique situation at the company?	
• Is this weakness a result of a unique situation in the industry?	
3. After meeting with the management team, those charged with governance, and the independent auditor, address whether the weakness(es) could have resulted from an illegal act.	
• Consider the need to conduct a formal investigation in the area to determine if the weakness(es) resulted from an illegal act.	
• Consider the need to engage a forensic accountant/auditor to review the situation if any fraud or illegal activity is suspected.	
• If an illegal act is suspected, work expeditiously to determine if such an act occurred. If confirmed, notify those charged with governance or other relevant parties.	
4. Consult experts from outside the organization about the weakness(es) and the steps necessary to be taken to correct it or them.	

(continued)

Sample Questions	Comments
Independent Auditor	
5. Work with management to develop a plan to correct the weakness(es):	
• Identify metrics that can be reported to internal and external parties on the progress being made in correcting the weakness(es).	
6. Provided the company has corrected its internal control weakness successfully, consider whether to engage the independent auditor to issue a separate report on the elimination of the weakness in internal control over financial reporting.	
Additional Considerations	
1. Review with management its plan to communicate to key stakeholders (investors, regulators, or employees) the results of the adverse opinion, if appropriate.	
2. Review with management its plan to reassure key stakeholders about the findings and corrective action plans (if applicable).	
3. Review with management its communications plan for the business press who might be interested in the company's plans to correct the weakness(es) noted (if applicable).	
4. Inquire of management if they have considered other potential implications of the adverse report. For example, consider whether the adverse report could have an impact on:	
• Compliance with debt covenants	
• Partnership or alliance agreements, contracts with suppliers or customers	
• Other parties that could have an interest in the company	

PART III: Performance Evaluation

Chapter 16

Evaluating the Internal Audit Function: Questions to Consider

> **Overview:** The audit committee, including the Chief Audit Executive (CAE), has the responsibility to oversee and evaluate the internal audit function. This includes ensuring the internal audit function is independent and objective in order to perform its work effectively across the organization to provide the audit committee with an assessment on the state of the organization's risk, control, governance, and monitoring activities. In discharging this responsibility, the audit committee should answer a series of questions about the quality and performance of the internal audit function, and should obtain input from others in the organization including management and independent auditor.
>
> **Note:** The Institute of Internal Auditors (IIA) establishes standards for the internal audit profession and provides certifications in internal auditing. The International Standards for the Professional Practice of Internal Auditing (standards) provide guidance for the conduct of internal auditing at both the organizational and individual auditor levels. Internal audit functions that commit to adhering to these standards are required to establish a Quality Assurance and Improvement program that includes both ongoing and periodic internal quality assessment reviews (QARs) and undergo an external QAR a minimum of once every five years.

> **Instructions for using this tool:** The sample questions included in this tool are only a starting point for evaluating the performance and effectiveness of the internal audit function. Audit committee members should ask follow-up questions as appropriate and required.

Evaluation of Internal Audit Team	Yes	No	N/A	Comments
1. Has the internal audit charter been evaluated to determine whether it is still current, conforms with IIA standards and reflects best practices?	☐	☐	☐	
2. Has the internal audit function fulfilled the responsibilities as defined within the charter?	☐	☐	☐	
3. a. Does the internal audit function maintain a quality assurance and improvement program?	☐	☐	☐	
b. Has the internal audit function conducted the external QAR required by IIA standards in the last five years?	☐	☐	☐	

(continued)

Evaluation of Internal Audit Team	Yes	No	N/A	Comments
4. Is the CAE reporting relationship appropriate to provide adequate independence to fulfill the CAE's role and meet the needs of the organization? Best practice is the CAE reporting functionally to the audit committee and administratively to the CEO.	☐	☐	☐	
5. Does the organization's executive leadership support and value the work performed by the internal audit function?	☐	☐	☐	
6. If the internal audit function is outsourced: *a.* Are the areas outsourced appropriately?	☐	☐	☐	
b. Is sufficient monitoring in place to assure the quality of the outsourced function?	☐	☐	☐	
7. Are the internal auditors independent and objective both in fact and appearance?	☐	☐	☐	
8. Is the internal audit function's size, budget, and structure adequate to meet its established objectives?	☐	☐	☐	
9. Does the internal audit function stay abreast of relevant updates such as COSO framework, IFRS, and GAAP?	☐	☐	☐	
10. Has the internal audit function addressed all scope limitations and access issues?	☐	☐	☐	
11. Do the internal auditors feel comfortable raising issues that could reflect negatively on management?	☐	☐	☐	
12. Are the technical knowledge and experience levels of the internal audit function staff sufficient to ensure that duties are performed appropriately?	☐	☐	☐	
13. Is the internal audit function's work planned appropriately to address the risks of the organization and focused on the right areas of high risk, judgment, and sensitivity?	☐	☐	☐	

Evaluation of Internal Audit Team	Yes	No	N/A	Comments
14. Does the internal audit function's work encompass a good balance between operational and financial areas?	☐	☐	☐	
15. Does the internal audit function appear to be using its time and resources effectively and efficiently in performing the annual internal audit plan?	☐	☐	☐	
16. Did the internal audit function consider changes in the independent auditor leadership and staffing when preparing the annual audit plan around financial areas?	☐	☐	☐	
17. Was the internal audit function's involvement in the annual independent audit effective?	☐	☐	☐	
18. Did the internal audit function provide constructive observations, implications, and recommendations in areas needing improvement?	☐	☐	☐	
19. Does management respond in an appropriate and timely fashion to significant recommendations and comments made by the internal audit function?	☐	☐	☐	
20. Does the internal audit function have adequate on-boarding and training programs to incorporate new staff members quickly?	☐	☐	☐	
21. Does the internal audit function have continuing education programs and leadership training to grow and develop staff?	☐	☐	☐	
22. Did the internal audit function address any feedback satisfactorily from the audit committee or senior management?	☐	☐	☐	
23. Could more be done in the future to maximize the internal audit function's effectiveness and efficiency? If yes, please provide comments.	☐	☐	☐	

Other Comments, Further Questions				

Chapter 17

Evaluating the Independent Auditor: Questions to Consider

Overview: As a best practice, the audit committee has the responsibility to hire, compensate, fire, and evaluate the independent auditor (auditor). In discharging this responsibility, the audit committee should answer a series of questions about the quality and performance of the auditor, and should obtain input from others in the organization, including management and internal audit.

Instructions for using this tool: The sample questions included in this tool are only a starting point for evaluating the performance and effectiveness of the auditor. Audit committee members should ask follow-up questions as appropriate and required.

Questions for Audit Committee Members

Evaluation of the Independent Auditor	Yes	No	N/A	Comments
Quality of Resources and Services				
1. Does the audit team have the knowledge and skills necessary to meet the company's audit requirements, including specialized skills and industry knowledge? (Consider abilities of the partners, managers, and fieldwork leaders, and level of access to specialized expertise).	☐	☐	☐	
2. Does the auditor identify and discuss the appropriate risks considered in the planning of the audit, including tone at the top, fraud, governance matters, and risk of management override of controls?	☐	☐	☐	
3. Are you satisfied with the auditor's planning, execution, and communication related to the audit, including the scope, nature, extent, and timing of the testing performed?	☐	☐	☐	

(continued)

Evaluation of the Independent Auditor	Yes	No	N/A	Comments
Quality of Resources and Services				
4. Does the firm leverage the work performed by internal audit, management, or both for the audit of internal control over financial reporting when determining the work needed for the audit of the financial statements?	☐	☐	☐	
5. Do the auditor's written reports to the audit committee cover all appropriate issues adequately, giving consideration to requirements such as GAAP and GAAS as well as elements required by the auditor contained in the audit committee charter?	☐	☐	☐	
6. Are the audit fees reasonable and sufficient in light of the quality of services provided, size and complexity of the company's business, and the risks facing the company and its industry?	☐	☐	☐	
Quality of Communications				
7. Does the auditor communicate issues openly, and in a complete and understandable way?	☐	☐	☐	
8. Does it appear that the auditor is free from undue influence by management, and that the auditor is comfortable raising issues that would reflect negatively on management?	☐	☐	☐	
9. Does the auditor take advantage of executive session appropriately by discussing any sensitive issues professionally, candidly, and in a timely manner?	☐	☐	☐	
10. Does the auditor communicate, or ensure that management communicates, relevant developments in accounting principles and auditing standards that could impact the company?	☐	☐	☐	

Evaluation of the Independent Auditor	Yes	No	N/A	Comments
Quality of Communications				
11. Does the auditor volunteer constructive observations, implications, and recommendations in areas needing improvement, particularly with respect to the company's internal controls over financial reporting?	☐	☐	☐	
Independence and Objectivity				
12. Considering all audit-related and nonaudit services performed by the auditor, are you satisfied that the auditor remains independent and objective both in fact and appearance?	☐	☐	☐	
13. Are you satisfied that the auditor reports all matters openly to the audit committee that might be thought to bear on the firm's independence?	☐	☐	☐	
14. Based on the open and informative nature of the auditor's answers to questions posed by the audit committee, do you feel confident that the auditor maintains appropriate objectivity and professional skepticism?	☐	☐	☐	
Final Evaluation				
15. Based on your assessment, would you rehire the auditor to conduct future audits? If yes, what changes would you make, if any? Notes:	☐	☐	☐	

Questions for Management and/or Internal Audit

Evaluation of the Independent Auditor	Yes	No	N/A	Comments
In addition to the questions above, following are questions the audit committee may ask of company personnel such as the CAE, CFO, controller, or general counsel, to assist in evaluating the performance of the auditor.				
1. Does the auditor work with internal audit to ensure the coordination of audit efforts to assure the completeness of coverage, reduction of redundant efforts, and the effective use of audit resources?	☐	☐	☐	
2. a. Are you satisfied with the knowledge, skills, and abilities of the staff assigned to do the audit work?	☐	☐	☐	
b. Are you satisfied with the performance of the engagement leadership assigned, including the partner(s), manager(s), and fieldwork leaders?	☐	☐	☐	
3. Was cooperative work with the auditor conducted in the spirit of professionalism and mutual respect?	☐	☐	☐	
4. a. Are you aware of any other information that might impair the independence of the audit firm?	☐	☐	☐	
b. Are you aware of any individuals on the audit team who might not be independent with respect to the company for whatever reason?	☐	☐	☐	
5. a. If the choice were yours, would you hire the firm to conduct future audits?	☐	☐	☐	
b. If so, what changes would you make, if any?	☐	☐	☐	

Other Comments, Further Questions				

Chapter 18

Conducting an Audit Committee Self-Evaluation: Questions to Consider

> **Overview:** The audit committee should conduct a self-evaluation on an annual basis to evaluate its performance and effectiveness. Audit committee members should answer a series of questions independently to complete their self-evaluations. The entire audit committee should discuss the answers and plan for further action as appropriate.

> **Instructions for using this tool:** The sample questions included in this tool are only a starting point to evaluating the performance and effectiveness of the audit committee. These questions should be completed anonymously by each audit committee member prior to the audit committee meeting, and the entire committee should discuss the responses.

Audit Committee Self-Evaluation	Yes	No	N/A	Comments
1. Does the audit committee have a charter that covers all standard best practices? Has the charter been reviewed annually? For a listing of standard best practices for an audit committee charter, see chapter 3, "Audit Committee Charter Matrix," in this toolkit.	☐	☐	☐	
2. Is the audit committee charter used as a document to guide the committee in its efforts and to help guide the committee's agenda? Have all elements been covered throughout the fiscal year?	☐	☐	☐	
3. Are the members educated appropriately on the company, its organizational structures, governance and internal control environment, and current hot topics, as well as the company's risk profile?	☐	☐	☐	
4. Are the members independent?	☐	☐	☐	
5. Does each member possess an appropriate level of financial acumen?	☐	☐	☐	

(continued)

Audit Committee Self-Evaluation	Yes	No	N/A	Comments
6. Is there a sufficient mix of necessary skill sets and knowledge among the audit committee members?	☐	☐	☐	
7. Do the members convey the appropriate tone at the top?	☐	☐	☐	
8. Do audit committee members participate in some form of continuing education to stay abreast of changes in the relevant financial accounting and reporting, regulatory, and ethics areas?	☐	☐	☐	
9. Are the audit committee's meeting packages complete and given to committee members with enough lead time? Do the packages include the right information to allow meaningful discussion?	☐	☐	☐	
10. Are the audit committee meetings well organized, efficient, effective, and of the appropriate length? Do they occur often enough to allow discussion of issues that are relevant to and consistent with the audit committee's responsibilities?	☐	☐	☐	
11. Do the minutes and reports to the full board reflect the significant activities, actions, and recommendations of the committee?	☐	☐	☐	
12. Does the audit committee have open access to management, internal audit, and independent auditors? Do committee members have open, honest, and effective communication with management, the internal auditors, and the independent auditors? Is the audit committee able to challenge management, the internal auditors, and the independent auditors with its own view on issues as appropriate?	☐	☐	☐	
13. Are differences of opinion on issues resolved to the satisfaction of the entire audit committee?	☐	☐	☐	

Audit Committee Self-Evaluation	Yes	No	N/A	Comments
14. Is the committee cognizant of the line between oversight and management, and does it endeavor to respect that line?	☐	☐	☐	
15. Does the audit committee have a clear definition of the services the independent auditors are allowed to perform in order to maintain independence? Does the committee approve all allowed services of the independent auditors in advance?	☐	☐	☐	
16. Does the audit committee review the independent auditors' reports to ensure the auditors maintain their independence? Does the committee review the reports at least annually?	☐	☐	☐	
17. Does the audit committee engage in the hiring and evaluation of the chief audit executive (CAE)? Does the committee provide feedback to the CAE? Does the committee do its part to ensure the quality and objectivity of the internal audit team?	☐	☐	☐	
18. Does the committee receive the appropriate level of information to evaluate the soundness of the organization's internal control environment?	☐	☐	☐	
19. Does the committee engage outside experts as appropriate?	☐	☐	☐	
20. Does the committee conduct executive sessions in a manner that offers a safe haven to the individual? During executive sessions, does the audit committee ask tough and necessary questions, evaluate the answers, and pursue issues that might arise to a satisfactory resolution?	☐	☐	☐	
21. Do the members challenge the chair as appropriate?	☐	☐	☐	

(continued)

Audit Committee Self-Evaluation	Yes	No	N/A	Comments
22. Does the audit committee receive constructive 360-degree feedback from management, internal and independent auditors, and peer groups?	☐	☐	☐	
23. Are the organization's overall governance and internal controls, including financial reporting processes, stronger as a result of management's interactions with the audit committee?	☐	☐	☐	

Other Comments, Further Questions				

PART IV: Other Tools

Chapter 19
Enterprise Risk Management:
A Primer on the COSO Framework

Overview: Historically, risk management efforts in most organizations have been focused on preventing losses of physical or financial assets at the operational level. Since the passage of the Sarbanes-Oxley Act (the Act), much attention has been paid to risk in the context of the requirements of SOX Section 404 and management's responsibility for maintaining an effective system of internal control over financial reporting (ICFR).

These efforts directed to compliance with these requirements have been critical to restoring the credibility of financial reporting and corporate disclosure in the wake of the high-profile scandals that precipitated SOX, as well as subsequent failures in the late 2000s. However, many corporate failures are not the result of misconduct. Rather, they are the result of organizations managing risk ineffectively at the strategic level.

Enterprise risk management is an attempt to manage risk in a comprehensive manner that is aligned with the strategic direction of the organization and integrated with the everyday management of the business. Many companies, their boards, and audit committees view risk management from this strategic perspective, and consider risk management oversight to be a critical element of governance.

This chapter is intended to give boards an overview of enterprise risk management, its opportunities and limitations, the relationship between enterprise risk management and internal control, and the roles and responsibilities for risk management in the organization. Enterprise risk management is a management responsibility, subject to oversight of the board of directors. It does not involve external audit attestation.

Audit committee role: It should be noted that there is no regulatory mandate for implementation of enterprise risk management. However, New York Stock Exchange Corporate Governance Rules require that the audit committees of listed companies have written charters stipulating committee responsibilities, including the duty to discuss risk assessment and risk management policies. Additionally, the SEC requires public companies to describe in the annual proxy the board of directors' role in the oversight of risk.

Enterprise Risk Management Primer—Basics of ERM and Its Relationship to Internal Control

In September 2004, the Committee of Sponsoring Organizations (COSO)[1] of the National Commission on Fraudulent Financial Reporting of the Treadway Commission published a document called *Enterprise Risk Management—Integrated Framework*,[2] (ERM framework), which defined enterprise risk management as

> ... a process, effected by an entity's board of directors, management, and other personnel, applied in a strategy setting and across the enterprise, designed to identify potential events that may affect the entity, and manage risk to be within its risk appetite, to provide reasonable assurance regarding the achievement of entity objectives.

The ERM framework is geared toward achieving an entity's objectives, set forth in four categories.

1. Strategic: high-level goals, aligned with and supporting its mission
2. Operations: effective and efficient use of its resources
3. Reporting: reliability of reporting
4. Compliance: compliance with applicable laws and regulations

The COSO Enterprise Risk Management Framework consists of the following eight interrelated components:

1. *Internal Environment:* The internal environment sets the foundation for how risk is viewed and addressed by an entity's people, including risk philosophy and risk appetite, integrity and ethical values, and the environment in which they operate.

2. *Objective Setting:* Objectives must exist before management can identify potential risks affecting their achievement. Enterprise risk management ensures that management has in place a process to set objectives, that the chosen objectives support and align with the entity's mission, and that they are consistent with its risk appetite.

3. *Event Identification:* Internal and external events affecting the achievement of an entity's objectives must be identified, distinguishing between risks and opportunities.

4. *Risk Assessment:* Risks are analyzed, considering likelihood and impact, as a basis for how they should be managed. Risks are assessed on an inherent and residual basis.

5. *Risk Response:* Management selects risk responses—avoiding, accepting, reducing or sharing risk—developing a set of actions to align risks with the entity's risk tolerances and risk appetite.

---

[1] The Committee of Sponsoring Organizations consists of the American Institute of CPAs (AICPA), the Institute of Management Accountants (IMA), the Institute of Internal Auditors (IIA), Financial Executives International (FEI), and the American Accounting Association (AAA).

[2] The COSO publication *Enterprise Risk Management—Integrated Framework* (Product Code Number 990015), may be purchased through the AICPA store at www.cpa2biz.com. The proceeds from the sale of this publication are used to support the continuing work of COSO.

6. *Control Activities:* Policies and procedures are established and implemented to help ensure the risk responses are carried out effectively.

7. *Information and Communication:* Relevant information is identified, captured, and communicated in a form and timeframe that enable people to carry out their responsibilities. Effective communication also occurs in a broader sense, flowing down, across, and up the entity.

8. *Monitoring:* The entire ERM process is monitored, and modifications are made as necessary. Monitoring is accomplished through ongoing management activities, separate evaluations, or both.

Enterprise risk management is not a serial process, but a multi-directional iterative process, with the eight components impacting each other. Likewise the eight components will not function identically in every entity. Application in small and medium- sized companies is likely to be less formal and less structured.

The components are the criteria for the effectiveness of enterprise risk management. When each of the eight components is determined to be present and functioning effectively, and risk has been brought within the entity's risk appetite, management and the board of directors have reasonable assurance that they understand the extent to which each of the four categories' objectives is being achieved by the entity.

Relationship Between COSO Enterprise Risk Management—Integrated Framework and Internal Control—Integrated Framework

In the 20 years since COSO released its *Internal Control—Integrated Framework* (the original framework), business and operating environments have changed dramatically, becoming increasingly complex, technologically driven, and global. At the same time, stakeholders are more engaged, seeking greater transparency and accountability for the integrity of systems of internal control that support business decisions and governance of the organization.

In 2013, COSO published the updated *Internal Control—Integrated Framework* (framework). COSO believes the framework will enable organizations to effectively and efficiently develop and maintain systems of internal control that can enhance the likelihood of achieving the entity's objectives and adapt to changes in the business and operating environments.

The 2004 ERM framework and the 2013 framework are intended to be complementary, and neither supersedes the other. Yet, while these frameworks are distinct and provide a different focus, they do overlap. The ERM framework encompasses internal control, with several portions of the text of the original *Internal Control—Integrated Framework* reproduced. Consequently, the ERM framework remains viable and suitable for designing, implementing, conducting, and assessing enterprise risk management.

Internal Control—Integrated Framework remains in place as a tool for evaluating internal control by itself and is also encompassed within enterprise risk management. The relationship between internal control and enterprise risk management is possibly best captured by the phrase "you can have effective internal control without effective enterprise risk management, but you cannot have effective enterprise risk management without effective internal control."

Internal control is an integral part of enterprise risk management, which is a broader conceptual tool, expanding and elaborating on internal control, focusing more fully on risk, especially as it relates to strategic considerations.

These key areas are included in the ERM framework to expand on the internal control framework:

- *Objectives:* The internal control framework specifies three categories of objectives—operations, financial reporting, and compliance. The ERM framework adds strategic objectives and expands the reporting objective to cover all reports developed and disseminated internally or externally, and expands the scope to cover non-financial information.

- *Environment:* The ERM framework discusses an entity's risk management philosophy, which is the set of shared beliefs and attitudes characterizing how an entity considers risks, and reflects its culture and operating style.

- *Risk appetite and risk tolerance:* Risk appetite, set by management, with oversight by the board of directors, is a broad-based conceptualization of the amount of risk that an entity is willing to take to achieve its goals. Often expressed as the desired or acceptable balance among growth, risk and return, or as stakeholder value added measures, an entity's risk appetite serves as a guidepost for making strategic choices and resource allocation decisions that are consistent with its established risk appetite.

  The risk appetite is supported by more specific risk tolerances that reflect the degree of acceptable variation in executing business activities. Risk tolerances are usually best measured in the same units as the objectives that they relate to, and are aligned with the overall risk appetite.

- *Portfolio view of risk:* The ERM framework also introduced the notion of taking a portfolio view of risk—looking at the composite of entity risks from a portfolio perspective. A portfolio view of risk can be depicted in a variety of ways. A portfolio view may be gained from looking at major risks or event categories across business units, or by focusing on risk for the company as a whole using capital, operating earnings or other metrics. Taking a portfolio view enables management to determine whether it remains within its risk appetite, or whether additional risks should be accepted in some areas in order to enhance returns.

- *Risk assessment and response:* In addition to considering risk from a portfolio perspective, the ERM framework calls attention to interrelated risks, where a single event or decision may create multiple risks.

  The framework also identifies four categories of risk response that are taken into consideration by management in looking at inherent risks and achieving a residual risk level that is in line with the entity's risk tolerances and overall risk appetite.

  There are four risk response categories.

  —*Acceptance:* No action is taken to affect risk likelihood or impact.

—*Avoidance:* Exiting the activities giving rise to risk; may involve exiting a product line, declining expansion to a new geographical market, or selling a division.

—*Reduction:* Action is taken to reduce risk likelihood, impact, or both; typically involves many everyday business decisions.

—*Sharing:* Reducing risk likelihood or impact by transferring or otherwise sharing a portion of the risk; common techniques include purchasing insurance products, forming joint ventures, engaging in hedging transactions, or outsourcing an activity.

Other Key Terms in Enterprise Risk Management

There are several additional terms that you will hear when discussing enterprise risk management. They are described in the rest of this section.

Inherent and residual risk: Management needs to consider both inherent and residual risk. Inherent risk is the risk to the achievement of entity objectives in the absence of any actions management might take to alter either the risk's likelihood or impact. Residual risk is the risk to the achievement of objectives that remains after management's responses have been developed and implemented. Risk analysis is applied first to inherent risk. Once risk responses have been developed, as discussed below, management then considers residual risk. Assessing inherent risk in addition to residual risk can assist the organization in understanding the extent of risk responses needed.

Event identification techniques: An entity's event identification methodology may comprise a combination of techniques and supporting tools ranging from interactive group workshops and process flow analysis, to technology-based inventories of potential events. These tools and techniques look to past trends, such as loss histories, as well as to the future. Some are industry specific; most are derived from a common approach. They vary widely in levels of sophistication, and most companies use a combination of techniques.

Risk assessment techniques: Risk assessment methodologies comprise a combination of qualitative and quantitative techniques. The use of interviews or group assessment of the likelihood or impact of future events is an example of the application of qualitative risk assessment. Quantitative techniques include probabilistic and non-probabilistic models. Probabilistic models are based on certain assumptions about the likelihood of future events. Non-probabilistic models, such as scenario-planning, sensitivity measures, and stress tests, attempt to estimate the impact of events without quantifying an associated likelihood.

Risk analysis techniques: As part of risk analysis, the organization analyzes the significance of risks to the achievement of objectives and sub-objectives. Organizations may address significance further by using the following criteria:

- *Likelihood and impact of risk occurring:* "Likelihood" and "impact" are commonly used terms, although some entities use instead "probability," "severity," "seriousness," or "consequence." Likelihood represents the possibility that a given event will occur, while impact represents its effect. Sometimes the words take on more specific meaning, with likelihood indicating the possibility that a given risk will occur in qualitative terms such as high, medium, and low. The word probability indicates a quantitative measure such as a percentage, frequency of occurrence, or other numerical metric.

- *Velocity or speed to impact upon occurrence of the risk:* Risk velocity refers to the pace with which the entity is expected to experience the impact of the risk. For instance, a manufacturer of consumer electronics may be concerned about changing customer preferences and compliance with radio frequency energy limits. Failing to manage either of these risks may result in significant erosion in the entity's value, even to the point of being put out of business. In this instance, changes in regulatory requirements develop much more slowly than do changes in customer preferences

- *Persistence or duration of time that an occurrence of the risk could affect the organization:* Certain risks are temporary in nature and others are more lasting. For example, the risk of a hurricane that briefly disrupts distribution has a shorter duration than the risk of a persistent shift in consumer demands for retailers to have an online presence. Additionally, those risks with a potentially high impact that have a low likelihood should be considered, avoiding the notion that such risks "couldn't happen here," as even low likelihood risks can occur. The importance of understanding risks assessed as having a low likelihood is greater when the potential impact of the risk might persist over a longer period of time. For instance, the long-term impact on the entity from environmental damage caused by the entity's actions may be viewed much differently than the long-term impact of losing technology processing in a manufacturing plant for several days.

Portfolio View of Residual Risk Example

The following example excerpted from the ERM framework summarizes ERM concepts.

> A company that manufactures and distributes inflatable rafts for personal recreational use held a management team retreat to brainstorm its key risks: changes in interest rates adversely impacting consumer demand; unexpected increase in raw materials prices; and the potential of a work stoppage. Taking a portfolio view, they established a measure for overall residual risk tolerance measured in terms of earnings per share.

> Management assessed the risks and developed risk responses to bring these key risks to within established limits. These responses included a hedging program to reduce the effect of interest rate fluctuations, executed at the corporate level; a negotiating strategy to reduce the likelihood of a work stoppage, executed at the business unit level; and long-term contracts for raw materials to minimize the impact of price fluctuations, also executed at the entity level.

Roles and Responsibilities

Everyone in the organization has some role to play in enterprise risk management.

Board of Directors: Authority for key decisions involving strategic direction, broad-based resource allocation and setting high-level objectives is reserved for the board. Ensuring that objectives are met, determining that resources are utilized effectively, and ascertaining that risks are managed appropriately in the execution of strategy are key functions of the board and its committees.

The board's role in providing oversight of enterprise risk management in an organization includes these five responsibilities:

1. Influencing and concurring with the entity's risk philosophy and risk appetite
2. Determining that overall strategy and strategic decisions are in alignment with the entity's risk appetite and philosophy
3. Ascertaining the extent to which management has established effective enterprise risk management in the organization
4. Reviewing the entity's portfolio view of risk and considering it in relation to the entity's risk appetite
5. Being apprised of the most significant risks and ascertaining whether management is responding appropriately

Internal Audit: The role of internal audit in enterprise risk management is twofold. In addition to identifying and evaluating risk exposures, internal audit activities, according to *International Standards for the Professional Practice of Internal Auditing*, must include monitoring and evaluating the effectiveness of the organization's risk management system. In this role, internal auditors may support management by providing assurance on the

- enterprise risk management processes, both design and function;
- effectiveness and efficiency of risk responses and related control activities; and
- completeness and accuracy of enterprise risk management reporting.

This responsibility for evaluating the effectiveness of the organization's risk management function requires the internal audit function to maintain its independence and objectivity with respect to this function. Accordingly, best practice from a corporate governance perspective would suggest that reporting responsibility for the risk function be a management responsibility that is separate from internal audit. That said, because of internal audit's position in the organization and its knowledge of risk assessment, internal audit team often is responsible for facilitating the ERM process. In the role of facilitator, internal audit can aid in maintaining its independence by communicating its role regularly to stakeholders, including the audit committee. The audit committee should monitor this structure to ensure that roles and responsibilities are understood, and internal audit is maintaining its independence.

Limitations of Enterprise Risk Management

Effective enterprise risk management will provide reasonable assurance to management and the board of directors regarding the achievement of an entity's objectives. However, achievement of objectives is affected by limitations inherent in any management process and the inherent uncertainty of all human endeavors.

The role and reality of human judgment in all aspects of management, including the selection of appropriate objectives, the inevitability of some degree of failure or error, and the possibility of collusion or management override of the process, are limiting factors that decrease the effectiveness of management-level decisions. Another important limitation that must be considered is the cost of various risk response alternatives in relation to their projected benefits.

Conclusion

This primer should have given you a sense of what is meant by enterprise risk management, and an understanding of the responsibilities of a board of directors and audit committee with respect to risk management within an organization.

While some risk management practices and techniques are complex and sophisticated, the overall concept of enterprise risk management is not. Essentially, COSO ERM is a robust comprehensive framework that organizations, their management, and boards can use to manage risks and opportunities effectively in line with strategic choices.

Much of enterprise risk management encompasses board and management responsibilities that previously may have been carried out intuitively or in a manner less comprehensive and systematic than is contemplated by an enterprise approach.

All organizations from small, single-unit entities to large multinationals face, myriad risks and opportunities in a rapidly changing world. Whether large or small, local or global, a more explicit, enterprise approach to risk management can help an organization maximize its opportunities while avoiding unnecessary pitfalls or surprises.

Enterprise Risk Management: A Tool for Strategic Oversight

The next chapter in this toolkit, chapter 20, "Enterprise Risk Management: A Tool for Strategic Oversight," contains a tool with questions modeled on the framework in the COSO framework, *Enterprise Risk Management—Integrated Framework.*

Chapter 20

Enterprise Risk Management: A Tool for Strategic Oversight

Overview: The tool in this chapter is created around the eight interrelated components of the *Committee of Sponsoring Organizations of the Treadway Commission* (COSO) Enterprise Risk Management (ERM) Framework.[1] Refer to chapter 19, "Enterprise Risk Management: A Primer on the COSO Framework," in this toolkit, for a discussion of the components.

When each of the eight components is determined to be effective in each of the four categories of objectives, the board of directors and management have reasonable assurance that they understand the extent to which the entity's strategic and operations objectives are being achieved and that the entity's reporting is reliable and applicable laws and regulations are being complied with.

Instructions for using this tool: Within each section is a series of questions that the audit committee should answer to verify that the components of enterprise risk management are present and functioning properly.

These questions should be discussed in an open forum with key line and staff managers as well as members of the financial management, risk management, and internal audit teams to ensure that the enterprise risk management function is operating as management represents.

Evaluation of the risk management process is not a one-time event, but is, rather, a continuous activity for the audit committee, which should always look for potential deficiencies, and should probe the responsible parties continually regarding risks and opportunities.

---

[1] The questions in this tool are adapted from *COSO Enterprise Risk Management—Integrated Framework* (Product Code Number 990015), published September 2004 by the Committee of Sponsoring Organizations. It may be purchased through the AICPA store at www.cpa2biz.com. The proceeds from the sale of this publication are used to support the continuing work of COSO.

COSO Framework	Yes	No	Not sure	Comments
Internal Environment				
1. Is the assignment of risk oversight mandated clearly? Ultimately, the board is responsible for overseeing risk management, but oversight of the risk management process is often delegated to a board committee such as the audit committee.	☐	☐	☐	
2. Is the organization's philosophy for managing risk articulated in a comprehensive code of conduct or in other policies that address acceptable business practices and expected behavior?	☐	☐	☐	
3. Is the risk appetite for the organization articulated formally in qualitative or quantitative terms?	☐	☐	☐	
4. Is the risk appetite consistent with the stated risk management philosophy and aligned with business strategy? Is it included in the strategic plan?	☐	☐	☐	
Objective Setting				
1. Has the board established high-level objectives that are consistent with the strategic direction and risk appetite for the organization?	☐	☐	☐	
2. Has management identified critical success factors, relevant performance measures, milestones, and risk tolerances for the achievement of the organization's strategic objectives?	☐	☐	☐	
3. Has management identified breakpoints or risk tolerances that will trigger broad discussion of the potential need for intervention or modification of strategy?	☐	☐	☐	
4. Has management established operations, reporting, and compliance objectives that are aligned with the overall strategic objectives?	☐	☐	☐	

COSO Framework	Yes	No	Not sure	Comments
Objective Setting				
5. Is a relevant and timely progress reporting mechanism in place to monitor implementation of the strategy?	☐	☐	☐	
Event Identification				
1. Has management employed a systematic approach in the identification of potential events that will affect the entity?	☐	☐	☐	
2. Is the categorization of events across the organization, vertically through operating units, by type (including internal, external, and strategic) or by objective appropriate to the organization?	☐	☐	☐	
3. Has management included high impact, low likelihood events in its portfolio of events for assessment?	☐	☐	☐	
Risk Assessment				
1. Has management conducted a systematic assessment of the likelihood, impact, velocity, and persistence of all events with the potential for significant impact on the entity? The risk events should be assessed individually and not be aggregated into categories for assessment and reporting.	☐	☐	☐	
2. Has management considered sufficiently the interdependency of potentially related events in its event identification and risk assessment process?	☐	☐	☐	
Risk Response				
1. Has management adopted an appropriate and cost-effective array of risk responses, such as mitigation strategies, at the activity level of the organization to reduce inherent risks to levels in line with established risk tolerances?	☐	☐	☐	

(continued)

COSO Framework	Yes	No	Not sure	Comments
Risk Response				
2. Has management taken a portfolio view to assure that the selected risk responses have reduced the entity's overall residual risk to a level within the identified risk appetite for the organization?	☐	☐	☐	
Control Activities				
1. Has management implemented adequate control activities throughout the organization to assure that its risk responses are carried out properly and in a timely manner?	☐	☐	☐	
Information and Communication				
1. Do the organization's management information systems capture and provide reliable, timely, and relevant information sufficient to support effective enterprise risk management?	☐	☐	☐	
2. Have adequate communication vehicles been implemented to assure that relevant risk-related information is communicated by front-line employees upward in the organization and across business units or processes?	☐	☐	☐	
3. Are the portfolio of risks identified in the ERM process included in the strategic planning process?	☐	☐	☐	
Monitoring				
1. Are sufficient ongoing monitoring activities built into the organization's operating activities and performed on a real-time basis to allow for appropriate reaction to dynamically changing risk conditions?	☐	☐	☐	
2. Has evaluation of the ERM process, either in its entirety, or specific aspects, been given adequate consideration in the scope of internal audit work?	☐	☐	☐	

COSO Framework	Yes	No	Not sure	Comments
Monitoring				
3. Have all deficiencies in risk management processes identified by internal audit, or as a result of ongoing monitoring activities, been communicated to the appropriate levels of management, the board, or both?	☐	☐	☐	
4. Do the board's agendas promote integration of risk issues with other agenda items such as strategy, organization, and finance?	☐	☐	☐	
5. Have all deficiencies and recommendations for improvement in risk management processes been addressed? Have appropriate corrective actions been taken?	☐	☐	☐	

Chapter 21

SEC Final Rule on Audit Committee Financial Experts*

> **Overview:** The purpose of this chapter is to provide audit committee members with excerpts of the SEC Final Rule "Disclosure Required by Sections 406 and 407 of the Sarbanes-Oxley Act of 2002," which defines the term "financial expert" and how that term applies to the audit committee, especially in relationship to required disclosures. Although private companies are not required to comply with these rules, implementing the rules would be a best practice and would strengthen the board's governance around the financial reporting process. In addition, private companies that plan on becoming public companies should consider implementing these rules.

A. Audit Committee Financial Experts

1. Title of the Expert

We agree that the term "financial" may not completely capture the attributes referenced in Section 407, given the provision's focus on accounting and auditing expertise and the fact that traditional "financial" matters extend to capital structure, valuation, cash flows, risk analysis and capital-raising techniques. Furthermore, several recent articles on the proposals have noted that many experienced investors and business leaders with considerable financial expertise would not necessarily qualify as financial experts under the proposed definition.[1] We have decided to use the term "audit committee financial expert" in our rules implementing Section 407 instead of the term "financial expert."[2] This term suggests more pointedly that the designated person has characteristics that are particularly relevant to the functions of the audit committee, such as: a thorough understanding of the audit committee's oversight role, expertise in accounting matters as well as understanding of financial statements, and the ability to ask the right questions to determine whether the company's financial statements are complete and accurate. The new rules include a definition of the term "audit committee financial expert."[3]

---

* This material is excerpted from SEC Final Rule "Disclosure Required by Sections 406 and 407 of the Sarbanes-Oxley Act of 2002," Release Nos. 33-8177; 34-47235, March 28, 2003, with correction release. See http://www.sec.gov/rules/final/33-8177.htm for text of the complete rule. Throughout the text "we" means the SEC.

[1] See Andrew R. Sorkin, "Back to School, but This One Is for Top Corporate Officials," NY Times, Sept. 3, 2002, Cassell Bryan-Low, "Defining Moment for SEC: Who is a financial expert," Wall Street Journal, Dec. 9, 2002, and Geoffrey Colvin, "Sarbanes & Co. Can't Want This: Under Reform Law, Alan Greenspan Would Not Qualify as a Board's Financial Expert," Fortune, Dec. 30, 2002.

[2] Throughout this release, we will refer to both "audit committee financial experts" and "financial experts" as appropriate in a particular context. For example, when discussing statutory provisions, we will continue to refer to financial experts. For purposes of the discussions in this release, the meanings of these terms are identical.

[3] See new Item 401(h)(2) of Regulation S-K, Item 401(e)(2) of Regulation S-B, Item 16A(b) of Form 20-F, and paragraph (8)(b) of General Instruction B to Form 40-F.

2. Disclosure of the Number and Names of Audit Committee Financial Experts

Under the rules that we adopted, a company must disclose that its board of directors has determined that the company either:

- has at least one audit committee financial expert serving on its audit committee; or
- does not have an audit committee financial expert serving on its audit committee.

A company disclosing that it does not have an audit committee financial expert must explain why it does not have such an expert. We continue to believe that disclosure of the name of the audit committee financial expert is necessary to benefit investors and to carry out the purpose of Section 407. Therefore, under the final rules, if a company discloses that it has an audit committee financial expert, it also must disclose the expert's name.

The final rules permit, but do not require, a company to disclose that it has more than one audit committee financial expert on its audit committee. Therefore, once a company's board determines that a particular audit committee member qualifies as an audit committee financial expert, it may, but is not required to, determine whether additional audit committee members also qualify as experts. Furthermore, if the company's board determines that at least one of the audit committee members qualifies as an expert, the company must accurately disclose this fact. It will not be appropriate for a company to disclose that it does not have an audit committee financial expert if its board has determined that such an expert serves on the audit committee.

3. Disclosure of Independence of Audit Committee Financial Experts

The final rules require a company to disclose whether its audit committee financial expert is independent of management. A number of commenters opposed this disclosure requirement as unnecessary, noting that Section 301 of the Sarbanes-Oxley Act mandates the Commission to direct the self-regulatory organizations to prohibit the listing of any company that does not require all of its audit committee members to be independent. However, not all Exchange Act reporting companies are listed on a national securities exchange or association.[4] We believe that investors in these companies would be interested in knowing whether the audit committee financial expert is independent of management.

To provide clarity, the final rules refer to the definition of "independent" used in Item 7(d)(3)(iv) of Schedule 14A.[5] This ensures that the term "independent" is used consistently in our rules.[6]

---

[4] As we note in our recent release proposing rules to implement Section 301 of the Sarbanes-Oxley Act, there are only 7,250 listed companies out of a total of approximately 17,000 reporting companies. See Release No. 33-8173 (Jan. 8, 2003).

[5] 17 CFR 240.101. That item currently relies on the definitions of "independent" in the listing standards of the New York Stock Exchange, the American Stock Exchange and the NASD. Under Section 10A(m) of the Exchange Act (as amended by Section 301 of the Sarbanes-Oxley Act), we recently proposed rules directing the national securities exchanges and national securities associations to prohibit the listing of any security of an issuer that, among other things, does not have an independent audit committee as that term is used in Section 10A(m)(3). See Release No. 33-8173 (Jan. 8, 2003). As a result of those proposals, the current references in Item 7(d)(3)(iv) of Schedule 14A may be amended. See *id.*

[6] For domestic issuers, the audit committee independence standard is found in new Regulation S-K Item 401(h)(1)(ii) (17 CFR 229.401(h)(1)(ii)) and Regulation S-B Item 401(e)(1)(ii) (17 CFR 228.401(e)(1)(ii)).

4. Definition of "Audit Committee Financial Expert"

a. Final Definition of "Audit Committee Financial Expert"

The final rules define an audit committee financial expert as a person who has the following attributes:

- An understanding of generally accepted accounting principles and financial statements;

- The ability to assess the general application of such principles in connection with the accounting for estimates, accruals and reserves;

- Experience preparing, auditing, analyzing or evaluating financial statements that present a breadth and level of complexity of accounting issues that are generally comparable to the breadth and complexity of issues that can reasonably be expected to be raised by the registrant's financial statements, or experience actively supervising one or more persons engaged in such activities;

- An understanding of internal controls and procedures for financial reporting; and

- An understanding of audit committee functions.[7]

Under the final rules, a person must have acquired such attributes through any one or more of the following:

(1) Education and experience as a principal financial officer, principal accounting officer, controller, public accountant or auditor or experience in one or more positions that involve the performance of similar functions;

(2) Experience actively supervising a principal financial officer, principal accounting officer, controller, public accountant, auditor or person performing similar functions;

(3) Experience overseeing or assessing the performance of companies or public accountants with respect to the preparation, auditing or evaluation of financial statements; or

(4) Other relevant experience.[8]

d. Discussion of Significant Modifications to the Proposed Definition of Financial Expert[9]

As already discussed, we have decided to use the term audit committee financial expert rather than financial expert in the final rules. We also have reorganized the components of the definition to make it easier to read and to emphasize, by including them in the first part of the definition, the attributes that an audit committee financial expert must possess. The second part of the definition discusses the means by which a person must acquire the necessary attributes.

---

[7] See new Item 401(h)(2) of Regulation S-K, Item 401(e)(2) of Regulation S-B, Item 16A(b) of Form 20-F and paragraph (8)(b) of General Instruction B to Form 40-F.

[8] See new Item 401(h)(3) of Regulation S-K, Item 401(e)(3) of Regulation S-B, Item 16A(c) of Form 20-F and paragraph (8)(c) of General Instruction B to Form 40-F.

[9] Ed note: Items B and C of this list have been omitted.

Proposed attributes of a financial expert.

    i.   The financial expert must have an understanding of generally accepted accounting principles and financial statements.

In response to comments, we have added an instruction to clarify that, with respect to foreign private issuers, the audit committee financial expert's understanding must be of the generally accepted accounting principles used by the foreign private issuer in preparing its primary financial statements filed with the Commission.[10] Our rules require foreign private issuers that do not prepare their primary financial statements in accordance with U.S. generally accepted accounting principles to include a reconciliation to those principles in the financial statements that they file with the Commission. Although an understanding of reconciliation to U.S. generally accepted accounting principles would be helpful, we believe that the proper focus of audit committee financial expertise is on the principles used to prepare the primary financial statement.

    ii.   The financial expert must have experience applying such generally accepted accounting principles in connection with the accounting for estimates, accruals and reserves that are generally comparable to the estimates, accruals and reserves, if any, used in the registrant's financial statements.

Several commenters were concerned that potential audit committee financial experts would not have experience with the unique and complex accounting for estimates, accruals and reserves in certain industries, such as the insurance industry, unless they have had direct previous experience in these industries. We have revised this attribute by eliminating the clause "that are generally comparable to the estimates, accruals and reserves, if any, used in the registrant's financial statements." We also have revised this attribute to state that the audit committee financial expert must have the ability to assess the general application of generally accepted accounting principles in connection with the accounting for estimates, accruals and reserves, rather than stating that the expert must have experience applying these principles.[11]

    iii.   The financial expert must have experience preparing or auditing financial statements that present accounting issues that are generally comparable to those raised by the registrant's financial statements.

The majority of commenters who thought that the proposed definition of "financial expert" was too restrictive focused on this attribute. We are convinced that the proposed requirement that an expert have direct experience preparing or auditing financial statements could impose an undue burden on some companies, especially small companies, that desire to have an audit committee financial expert. We therefore have broadened this attribute by requiring an audit committee financial expert to have experience "preparing, auditing, analyzing or evaluating" financial statements.[12]

---

[10] See new Instruction 3 to Item 401(h) of Regulation S-K, Item 401(e) of Regulation S-B, Instruction 3 to Item 16A of Form 20-F, and Note 3 to paragraph (8) of General Instruction B to Form 40-F.

[11] See new Item 401(h)(2)(ii) of Regulation S-K, Item 401(e)(2)(ii) of Regulation S-B, Item 16A(b)(2) of Form 20-F and paragraph (8)(b)(2) of General Instruction B to Form 40-F.

[12] See new Item 401(h)(2)(iii) of Regulation S-K, Item 401(e)(2)(iii) of Regulation S-B, Item 16A(b)(3) of Form 20-F and paragraph (8)(b)(3) of General Instruction B to Form 40-F.

We believe that our revisions properly capture the clear intent of the statute that an audit committee financial expert must have experience actually working directly and closely with financial statements in a way that provides familiarity with the contents of financial statements and the processes behind them. We recognize that many people actively engaged in industries such as investment banking and venture capital investment have had significant direct and close exposure to, and experience with, financial statements and related processes. Similarly, professional financial analysts closely scrutinize financial statements on a regular basis. They therefore would be well prepared to diligently and zealously question management and the company's auditor about the company's financial statements. Effective audit committee members must have both the ability and the determination to ask the right questions. Therefore, we have broadened this attribute to include persons with experience performing extensive financial statement analysis or evaluation.

We also are convinced that a potential audit committee financial expert should be considered to possess this attribute by virtue of his or her experience actively supervising a person who prepares, audits, analyzes or evaluates financial statements. The term "active supervision" means that a person engaged in active supervision participates in, and contributes to, the process of addressing, albeit at a supervisory level, the same general types of issues regarding preparation, auditing, analysis or evaluation of financial statements as those addressed by the person or persons being supervised. We also mean that the supervisor should have experience that has contributed to the general expertise necessary to prepare, audit, analyze or evaluate financial statements that is at least comparable to the general expertise of those being supervised.

Finally, we are retaining, with clarification, the requirement that an audit committee financial expert have experience with financial statements that present accounting issues that are "generally comparable" to those raised by the registrant's financial statements. We therefore have modified the requirement to focus on the breadth and level of complexity of the accounting issues with which the person has had experience. We think that a company's board of directors will make the necessary assessment based on particular facts and circumstances. In making its assessment, the board should focus on a variety of factors such as the size of the company with which the person has experience, the scope of that company's operations and the complexity of its financial statements and accounting.

    iv.   A financial expert must have experience with internal controls and procedures for financial reporting.

We are substituting the term "understanding" for the term "experience."[13] In our view, it is necessary that the audit committee financial expert understand the purpose, and be able to evaluate the effectiveness, of a company's internal controls and procedures for financial reporting. It is important that the audit committee financial expert understand why the internal controls and procedures for financial reporting exist, how they were developed, and how they operate. Previous experience establishing or evaluating a company's internal controls and procedures for financial reporting can, of course, contribute to a person's understanding of these

---

[13] See new Item 401(h)(2)(iv) of Regulation S-K, Item 401(e)(2)(iv) of Regulation S-B, Item 16A(b)(4) of Form 20-F and paragraph (8)(b)(4) of General Instruction B to Form 40-F.

matters, but the attribute as rephrased properly focuses on the understanding rather than the experience.

> v.   A financial expert must have an understanding of audit committee functions.

We are adopting this attribute as proposed.

> Means of obtaining expertise.

We have revised the audit committee financial expert definition to state that a person must have acquired the five necessary attributes through any one or more of the following:

(1) Education and experience as a principal financial officer, principal accounting officer, controller, public accountant or auditor or experience in one or more positions that involve the performance of similar functions;

(2) Experience actively supervising a principal financial officer, principal accounting officer, controller, public accountant, auditor or person performing similar functions;

(3) Experience overseeing or assessing the performance of companies or public accountants with respect to the preparation, auditing or evaluation of financial statements; or

(4) Other relevant experience.[14]

We have eliminated the proposed requirement that an audit committee financial expert must have gained the relevant experience with a company that, at the time the person held such position, was required to file reports pursuant to Section 13(a) or 15(d) of the Exchange Act. Many private companies are contractually required to prepare audited financial statements that comply with generally accepted accounting principles. In addition, a potential expert may have gained relevant experience at a foreign company that is publicly traded in its home market but that is not registered under the Exchange Act.

We have added a provision in response to comments that experience overseeing or assessing the performance of companies or public accountants with respect to the preparation, auditing or evaluation of financial statements can provide a person with in-depth knowledge and experience of accounting and financial issues.

In addition, we have revised the last provision of this part of the proposed definition. The final rules state simply that a person may acquire the necessary attributes of an audit committee financial expert through other relevant experience, and no longer require the company to disclose the basis for the board's determination that a person has "similar expertise and experience."

---

[14] See new Item 401(h)(3) of Regulation S-K, Item 401(e)(3) of Regulation S-B, Item 16A(c) of Form 20-F and paragraph (8)(c) of General Instruction B to Form 40-F.

Under the final rules, if a person qualifies as an expert by virtue of possessing "other relevant experience," the company's disclosure must briefly list that person's experience.[15]

> Proposed factors to be considered in evaluating the education and experience of a financial expert.

The proposed definition of "financial expert" included a non-exclusive list of qualitative factors for a company's board to consider in assessing audit committee financial expert candidates. These factors focused on the breadth and level of a potential audit committee financial expert's experience, understanding and involvement in relevant activities, including the person's length of experience in relevant positions, and the types of duties held by such person in those positions. The fact that a person previously has served on an audit committee does not, by itself, justify the board of directors in "grandfathering" that person as an audit committee financial expert under the definition. Similarly, the fact that a person has experience as a public accountant or auditor, or a principal financial officer, controller or principal accounting officer or experience in a similar position does not, by itself, justify the board of directors in deeming the person to be an audit committee financial expert. In addition to determining that a person possesses an appropriate degree of knowledge and experience, the board must ensure that it names an audit committee financial expert who embodies the highest standards of personal and professional integrity. In this regard, a board should consider any disciplinary actions to which a potential expert is, or has been, subject in determining whether that person would be a suitable audit committee financial expert.

> Requirement that an audit committee financial expert possess all five required attributes.

Although Congress did not explicitly require us to incorporate all of the attributes listed in Section 407 of the Sarbanes-Oxley Act, it also did not limit us to consideration of those attributes. Congress obviously considered each of the listed attributes to be important. A definition of "audit committee financial expert" that leaves the meaning of the term entirely to the judgment of the board of directors would be highly subjective and could constitute an abrogation of our responsibilities under Section 407.

The Sarbanes-Oxley Act did not contemplate that a company could disclose that it has an audit committee financial expert by virtue of the fact that the audit committee members collectively possess all of the attributes of an expert; the statute directs us to issue rules to require a company to disclose whether or not its audit committee is comprised of "at least one member" who is a financial expert. Due to the statute's use of this specific language, there is no doubt that Congress had in mind individual experts and did not contemplate a "collective" expert.

---

[15] See new Instruction 2 to Item 401(h) of Regulation S-K, Item 401(e) of Regulation S-B and Item 16A of Form 20-F and Note 2 to paragraph (8) of General Instruction B to Form 40-F.

5. Safe Harbor from Liability for Audit Committee Financial Experts

Unlike the provisions of the Act that impose substantive requirements,[16] the requirements contemplated by Section 407 are entirely disclosure-based. We find no support in the Sarbanes-Oxley Act or in related legislative history that Congress intended to change the duties, obligations or liability of any audit committee member, including the audit committee financial expert, through this provision.

In the proposing release, we stated that we did not believe that the mere designation of the audit committee financial expert would impose a higher degree of individual responsibility or obligation on that person. Nor did we intend for the designation to decrease the duties and obligations of other audit committee members or the board of directors.

To codify this position, we are including a safe harbor in the new audit committee disclosure item to clarify that:

- A person who is determined to be an audit committee financial expert will not be deemed an "expert" for any purpose, including without limitation for purposes of Section 11 of the Securities Act,[17] as a result of being designated or identified as an audit committee financial expert pursuant to the new disclosure item;

- The designation or identification of a person as an audit committee financial expert pursuant to the new disclosure item does not impose on such person any duties, obligations or liability that are greater than the duties, obligations and liability imposed on such person as a member of the audit committee and board of directors in the absence of such designation or identification; and

- The designation or identification of a person as an audit committee financial expert pursuant to the new disclosure item does not affect the duties, obligations or liability of any other member of the audit committee or board of directors.[18]

This safe harbor clarifies that any information in a registration statement reviewed by the audit committee financial expert is not "expertised" unless such person is acting in the capacity of some other type of traditionally recognized expert. Similarly, because the audit committee financial expert is not an expert for purposes of Section 11,[19] he or she is not subject to a higher

---

[16] For example, the Sarbanes-Oxley Act requires the Commission to direct the self-regulatory organizations by rule to mandate the independence of all audit committee members of companies listed on national securities exchanges and associations. See Section 301 of the Sarbanes-Oxley Act. As another example, Section 402 of the Sarbanes-Oxley Act prohibits certain loans made by companies to their directors and executive officers.

[17] 15 U.S.C. §77k.

[18] See new Item 401(h)(4) of Regulation S-K, Item 401(e)(4) of Regulation S-B, Item 16A(d) of Form 20-F and paragraph (8)(d) of General Instruction B to Form 40-F. Although other audit committee members may look to the audit committee financial expert as a resource on certain issues that arise, audit committee members should work together to perform the committee's responsibilities. The safe harbor provides that other audit committee members may not abdicate their responsibilities.

[19] Section 11 of the Securities Act imposes liability for material misstatements and omissions in a registration statement, but provides a defense to liability for those who perform adequate due diligence. The level of due diligence required depends on the position held by a defendant and the type of information at issue. *Escott v. BarChris Construction Corp.*, 283 F. Supp. 643 (S.D.N.Y. 1968). The type of information can be categorized as either "expertised," which means information that is prepared or certified by an expert who is named in the registration statement, or "non-expertised." Similarly, a defendant can be characterized either as an "expert" or a "non-expert."

level of due diligence with respect to any portion of the registration statement as a result of his or her designation or identification as an audit committee financial expert.

In adopting this safe harbor, we wish to emphasize that all directors bear significant responsibility. State law generally imposes a fiduciary duty upon directors to protect the interests of a company's shareholders. This duty requires a director to inform himself or herself of relevant facts and to use a "critical eye" in assessing information prior to acting on a matter.[20]

6. Determination of a Person's Status as an Audit Committee Financial Expert

The Sarbanes-Oxley Act does not explicitly state who at the company should determine whether a person qualifies as an audit committee financial expert. We believe that the board of directors in its entirety, as the most broad-based body within the company, is best-equipped to make the determination.

7. Location of Audit Committee Financial Expert Disclosure

The Sarbanes-Oxley Act expressly states that companies must include the financial expert disclosure in their periodic reports required pursuant to Section 13(a) or 15(d) of the Exchange Act. The final rules that we are adopting require companies to include the new disclosure in their annual reports on Forms 10-K, 10-KSB, 20-F or 40-F. The requirement to provide the new audit committee disclosure item is included in Part III of Forms 10-K and 10-KSB, enabling a domestic company that voluntarily chooses to include this disclosure in its proxy or information statement to incorporate this information by reference into its Form 10-K or 10-KSB if it files the proxy or information statement with the Commission no later than 120 days after the end of the fiscal year covered by the Form 10-K or 10-KSB.[21]

8. Change in Item Number

We proposed to designate the audit committee financial expert disclosure requirement as new Item 309 of Regulations S-K and S-B.[22] However, existing Item 401 seems to be a more logical location for this requirement. Item 401 currently requires, among other things, a brief description of the business experience of each director. Therefore, we are designating the new disclosure item as Item 401(h) of Regulation S-K and Item 401(e) of Regulation S-B. The new item specifies that a company may choose to include the audit committee financial expert disclosure in its proxy or information statement if the company incorporates such information into its annual report as permitted by the instructions to Forms 10-K and 10-KSB.[23]

---

[20] See, for example, *Smith v. Van Gorkom*, 488 A.2d 858 (Del. 1985).

[21] See General Instruction E(3) to Form 10-KSB [17 CFR 249.310b] and General Instruction G(3) to Form 10-K [17 CFR 249.310].

[22] We had proposed to add new items to Forms 20-F and 40-F as well. Those item numbers have not changed.

[23] See new Instruction 1 to Item 401(h) of Regulation S-K and Item 401(e) of Regulation S-B.

Chapter 22
IFRS Implementation

Overview: Since 1999, the Financial Accounting Standards Board (FASB) has signaled its support for converging global accounting standards. In 2002, the FASB began working formally with the International Accounting Standards Board (IASB) to actively develop a set of high-quality, compatible accounting standards for use in both domestic and cross-border financial reporting. Since 2002, several major accounting standards have converged, including standards on business combinations, fair value measurement, and non-controlling interests. The end goal of the convergence project is to eliminate many of the differences that exist between U.S. Generally Accepted Accounting Principles (U.S. GAAP) and International Financial Reporting Standards (IFRS).

Although private companies in the United States are not required to utilize specific financial reporting standards such as U.S. GAAP, financial reporting by private companies is typically driven by the requirements of public companies. Therefore, as the move toward IFRS progresses for public company reporting, there will likely be a related impact on private company reporting.

In July of 2009, the IASB issued *International Financial Reporting Standards for Small and Medium-Sized Entities (IFRS for SMEs)* that are specifically designed for entities that publish general-purpose financial statements for external users and do not have public accountability. The guidance is essentially a condensed, simplified version of full IFRS that allows for reduced disclosure requirements and eased recognition and measurement requirements. Since then, the IASB issued a request for information in 2012 and an exposure draft of proposed amendments as part of a comprehensive review process in 2013.

However, even with the simplified version for private companies and the declining differences between U.S. GAAP and IFRS for public companies, significant differences still remain and thus create a challenge for an entity when implementing IFRS. This chapter provides a three-stage approach to implementation for consideration.

Audit committee role: The audit committee's responsibility is to stay abreast of emerging issues. A successful and efficient transition to IFRS requires the involvement of all departments that either contribute to or use financial information. These departments must work together to assess strategically the impact of transition, develop a detailed conversion plan, and align the necessary resources that will be needed to execute the conversion efficiently.

Implementation

The implementation of IFRS should not be viewed as a burdensome task, but rather as an opportunity to align the entity's accounting policies more closely with the economics of its transactions. In turn, the result is more accurate financial data than can be utilized readily by the entity, creditors, and vendors alike.

Stage 1: Assessment

The implementation process should be broken down into manageable segments. The first stage involves assessing the broad impact that transition to IFRS will have on the entity. This transition is not solely limited to financial reporting, but can also include business processes, income tax compliance, long-term contracts, and future strategic planning. A thorough review of the entity's accounting policies should be conducted and documented, then compared against the applicable IFRS standards for potential key accounting and disclosure differences. This process identifies the areas that may require additional information and substantial work to execute the conversion.

Because IFRS is a principles-based model, it can require substantial additional information disclosures regarding certain accounting policies. Some of the additional information may be readily available, while other data may need to be gathered. The amount of information and the time needed to gather such information needs to be addressed properly in the planning stage.

The conversion to IFRS will undoubtedly impact areas outside of the scope of accounting policies. Joint ventures or other business agreements that may have been designed to achieve non-consolidation under U.S. GAAP may require new evaluation with IFRS. This can lead previously unconsolidated entities to be consolidated in the future, and therefore add to the amount of financial information that the parent entity is required to report. This situation can be complicated further if the entity that was not required previously to be consolidated is still reporting under U.S. GAAP.

The implementation of IFRS will likely impact key financial performance measures as well. This will require effective communication of such changes to board members, shareholders, and other key stakeholders of the entity, such as financial institutions.

By far the most integral key to the initial conversion stage is effective project management. The ability to coordinate personnel from multiple departments and geographic jurisdictions with varying skill sets that needs to work concurrently on transitional projects is fundamental in the conversion process. There are many different aspects of the conversion process that need to be considered; therefore, proper and thorough planning is needed before any other progress can begin.

Stage 2: Conversion

Once planning and impact assessment have been achieved, the focus shifts to actual conversion. There are several approaches that can be utilized for selecting which IFRS policy to implement. An entity that has previously been reporting under U.S. GAAP may choose to focus on the differences between U.S. GAAP and IFRS and then modify existing GAAP accounting policies as necessary. On the other hand, an entity may view the conversion process as an opportunity to overhaul its accounting policies to reflect the economics of the entities transactions more properly. The IFRS policies are principles based, unlike U.S. GAAP policies, which are rules based, and therefore allow for more professional judgment.

When identifying the differences between U.S. GAAP and IFRS, there will be items of definitive differences as well as items that may differ potentially. Because of the flexibility in the principles-based approach to IFRS, there are often accounting policy options that management will need to analyze and evaluate. All individual line items of the financial statements should be scrutinized for definitive and potential differences. Once the differences have been identified, they will need to be quantified.

When quantifying the individual differences between U.S. GAAP and IFRS financial statement balances, it is important to document the differences thoroughly, as well as the methodology for calculating the converted balance. This is to ensure that there is appropriate evidence and documentation to meet future audit requirements. Furthermore, depending on the requirements of the applicable IFRS standard, disclosure of reconciliation between U.S. GAAP balances and IFRS balances may be required in the financial statements.

The use of specialists may be necessary in the conversion stage, depending on the entity's knowledge and resources. Particularly, the intricacies of tax law may require a specialist to advise on restructured tax planning or compliance matters. IFRS conversion specialists can be utilized also to advise on technical issues while mitigating the learning curve of inexperienced staff.

Once the differences have been identified and quantified, the entity should prepare a financial statement template that reflects the appropriate IFRS presentation. IFRS financial statement presentation differs not only in format from U.S. GAAP presentation, but also in disclosure requirements. In most cases, additional information that was not disclosed previously under U.S. GAAP will need to be disclosed under IFRS. These format changes and additional informational disclosures will alter the appearance of the financial statements.

Stage 3: Integration

During conversion, the entity's financial reporting process will undergo various changes. The accounting policies that the entity previously complied with under U.S. GAAP and the processes that the entity utilized will be altered to comply with IFRS. This will require the revised financial reporting processes and systems to be embedded into the daily operations of the entity. The initial conversion process may have been implemented manually. Once the initial conversion is complete, those processes will need to be refined and implemented into the systems that will support IFRS reporting in the future.

It is likely that some existing policies will be consistent before and after the conversion. For those policies that are not consistent, it will be necessary to disseminate the appropriate materials, such as white papers, and educate key employees on the changes. Such changes most likely will affect various other segments, such as budgeting and forecasting.

There may be some overlap between the conversion and integration stages. Documentation from the conversion procedures can be utilized in developing and testing the long-term reporting processes. The time to complete the integration stage will vary by entity, depending on the accounting policy changes made, and the integration process can be perfected as IFRS reporting progresses.

Conclusion

The number of countries adopting IFRS has been progressing steadily year after year. In 2011, Canadian and Indian companies began using IFRS, and in 2012 Mexico adopted IFRS. With the adoption trend growing, many feel that the United States is on pace to allow public companies to convert their financial statements as early as 2015, which would in all likelihood directly impact private company reporting as well. Adoption of IFRS can pose numerous challenges for public and private companies alike. However, the potential benefits include increased comparability, better transparency, and greater awareness from foreign investors.

Chapter 23

Resources for Audit Committees

Overview: There is a wealth of resources available online to assist audit committee members in discharging their responsibilities. This chapter provides a list of organizations and websites that contain resources for audit committee members to investigate.

Below is a sampling of organizations and websites that can assist audit committee members in learning more about their roles, responsibilities, and functions.

American Institute of Certified Public Accountants

www.aicpa.org

The American Institute of Certified Public Accountants (AICPA) is the national professional association for all certified public accountants. This includes CPAs working as independent auditors, accountants, or consultants in public practice, business and industry (including CFOs, controllers, and internal auditors), government, not-for-profit organizations, and the academic community.

The AICPA has developed this Audit Committee Toolkit to aid audit committee members in performing their functions. In addition, the AICPA produces publications on accounting and auditing, financial reporting, tax, technology, and many other relevant topics. Some additional online resources useful to audit committees include the following:

- Audit Committee Effectiveness Center and Matching System at www.aicpa.org/audcommctr

- Fraud Resource Center at www.aicpa.org/interestareas/forensicandvaluation/resources/fraudpreventiondetectionresponse/pages/fraud-prevention-detection-response.aspx

- Internal Control Interest Area at www.aicpa.org/InterestAreas/BusinessIndustryAnd-Government/Resources/CorporateGovernanceRiskManagementInternalControl/Pages/COSO_Integrated_Framework_Project.aspx

Association of Certified Fraud Examiners

www.acfe.com

The Association of Certified Fraud Examiners (ACFE) is a global professional organization dedicated to fighting fraud and white-collar crime. With chapters around the globe, the ACFE is networked to respond to the needs of antifraud professionals everywhere. It offers guidance on fraud prevention, detection, and investigation, as well as internal controls. The ACFE publishes the *Report to the Nations on Occupational Fraud and Abuse* body of research aimed at deepening knowledge and understanding of the tremendous financial impact of occupational fraud and abuse on businesses and organizations.

Association of International Certified Professional Accountants
www.cgma.org

The Association of International Certified Professional Accountants established the Chartered Global Management Accountant (CGMA) designation in January 2012. The CGMA's mission is to promote the science of management accounting on the global stage. The designation champions management accountants and the value they add to organizations. Relevant tools and resources supporting board and audit committee responsibilities are included within the vast library on their website.

Business Roundtable
www.businessroundtable.org

The Business Roundtable (BRT) is an association of chief executive officers of leading U.S. corporations. The BRT is committed to advocating public policies that foster vigorous economic growth, a dynamic global economy, and a well-trained and productive U.S. workforce essential for future competitiveness. The BRT's Corporate Governance Committee focuses on issues related to corporate governance and responsibilities, including accounting standards.

Center for Audit Quality
www.thecaq.org

The Center for Audit Quality (CAQ) is an autonomous, nonpartisan, nonprofit group based in Washington, D.C. It is governed by a Board that comprises leaders from public company auditing firms, the AICPA, and three members from outside the public company auditing profession. The CAQ is dedicated to enhancing investor confidence and public trust in the global capital markets. The "Audit Committee Annual Evaluation of the External Auditor" resource is designed to allow audit committees to evaluate the auditor's performance objectively.

Committee of Sponsoring Organizations of the Treadway Commission
www.coso.org

The Committee of Sponsoring Organizations of the Treadway Commission (COSO) is a voluntary private-sector organization dedicated to improving the quality of financial reporting through business ethics, effective internal controls, and corporate governance. Originally formed in 1985 to sponsor the National Commission on Fraudulent Financial Reporting, COSO has released numerous influential publications, including, in May 2013, *Internal Control—Integrated Framework*.

Conference Board
www.conference-board.com

The Conference Board is a global, independent membership organization that creates and disseminates knowledge about management and the marketplace to help businesses strengthen their performance and better serve society. The Conference Board conducts research, convene conferences, make forecasts, assess trends, publish information and analysis, and bring executives together to learn from one another. The Conference Board's Commission on Public Trust and Private Enterprise has proposed reforms to strengthen corporate compensation practices and help restore trust in America's corporations and capital markets.

Corporate Board Member
www.boardmember.com

Corporate Board Member magazine's website, Boardmember.com, serves as a central resource for officers and directors of publicly traded corporations, large private companies, and Global 1000 firms. Their resource center offers the full texts of *Corporate Board Member* magazine articles, as well as additional articles, tools, Webcasts, and interviews. Topics include corporate governance, strategic board trends and issues, executive and director compensation, audit committees, risk management, international and technology trends, investor relations, board education, and other critical topics facing today's directors and officers of publicly traded companies. The Corporate Board Member extends its governance leadership through an online resource center, conferences, roundtables, and timely research.

Ethics & Compliance Officers Association
www.theecoa.org

The Ethics & Compliance Officers Association (ECOA) is the professional association exclusively for individuals responsible for their organizations' ethics, compliance, and business conduct programs. The ECOA provides ethics officers with training and a variety of conferences and meetings for exchanging best practices in a frank, candid manner.

Ethics Resources Center
www.ethics.org

The Ethics Resources Center (ERC) is a nonprofit, nonpartisan research organization, dedicated to independent research that advances high ethical standards and practices in public and private institutions, including a focus on ethics and compliance aspects of the federal government. Their mission is to promote ethical leadership worldwide by providing leading-edge expertise and services through research, education, and partnerships on current and emerging issues. The ERC's resources on business and organizational ethics are especially useful.

Financial Executives International
www.financialexecutives.org

Financial Executives International (FEI) is a professional association for senior level financial executives, including chief financial officers, vice-presidents of finance, controllers, treasurers, and tax executives. The FEI provides peer networking opportunities, emerging issues alerts, personal and professional development, and advocacy services.

GMI Ratings
www3.gmiratings.com

GMI Ratings was formed in 2010 through the merger of three independent companies: The Corporate Library, GovernanceMetrics International, and Audit Integrity. Drawing on the shared vision and intellectual capital of its predecessor firms, GMI Ratings emerged as a clear leader in the understanding of risks affecting the performance of public companies worldwide. Today, GMI Ratings provides institutional investors, insurers, and corporate decision-makers the most extensive coverage of environmental, social, governance, and accounting-related risks.

Harvard Business School's Corporate Governance
www.exed.hbs.edu

Harvard Business School's Corporate Governance website is a comprehensive overview of research, educational programs, and other activities at Harvard Business School aimed at providing new frameworks for thought and practice in the interrelated areas of corporate governance, leadership, and values. It includes links to the ongoing workshop series, background papers, research programs, executive education programs, viewpoints on key issues published in the national press, faculty comments in the media, and an online forum for exchanging views on emerging issues.

Institute of Internal Auditors
www.theiia.org

The Institute of Internal Auditors (IIA) is an international professional organization that meets the needs of a worldwide body of internal auditors. IIA focuses on issues and advocacy in internal auditing, governance and internal control, IT audit, education, and security worldwide. The Institute provides internal audit practitioners, executive management, boards of directors, and audit committees with standards, guidance, best practices, training, tools, certification, executive development, research, and technological guidance for the profession.

International Federation of Accountants
www.ifac.org

The International Federation of Accountants (IFAC) is the global organization for the accountancy profession dedicated to serving the public interest by strengthening the profession and contributing to the development of strong international economies. Its mission is to serve the public interest by contributing to the development of high-quality standards and guidance; facilitating the adoption and implementation of high-quality standards and guidance; contributing to the development of strong professional accountancy organizations and accounting firms and to high-quality practices by professional accountants, and promoting the value of professional accountants worldwide; and speaking out on public interest issues.

IT Governance Institute

www.itgi.org

Established by the Information Systems Audit and Control Association and Foundation (ISACA) in 1998, the IT Governance Institute (ITGI) exists to assist enterprise leaders in understanding and guiding the role of IT in their organizations. ITGI helps senior executives to ensure that IT goals align with those of the business, deliver value, and perform efficiently while IT resources are allocated properly to support business goals, optimize business investment in IT, and manage IT-related risk and opportunities appropriately through original research, symposia, and electronic resources. ITGI helps ensure that boards and executive management have the tools and information they need to manage the IT function effectively.

National Association of Corporate Directors

www.nacdonline.org

Founded in 1977, the National Association of Corporate Directors (NACD) is the premier educational, publishing, and consulting organization in board leadership, and the only membership association for boards, directors, director-candidates, and board advisers. The NACD promotes and advances exemplary board leadership through high professional board standards; creates forums for peer interaction; enhances director effectiveness; asserts the policy interests of directors; conducts research; and educates boards and directors concerning traditional and cutting-edge issues.

New York Stock Exchange

https://nyse.nyx.com/

The New York Stock Exchange (NYSE) is a not-for-profit corporation that provides a self-regulated marketplace for the trading of financial instruments. Its goal is to add value to the capital-raising and asset-management processes by providing the highest-quality and most cost-effective trading environment. The NYSE works to promote confidence in and understanding of the financial trading process, and serves as a forum for discussion of relevant national and international policy issues. The NYSE has taken a leadership role in corporate governance issues through its participation in the Blue Ribbon Committee on Improving the Effectiveness of Corporate Audit Committees and, more recently, in its formation of the NYSE Corporate Responsibility and Listing Standards Committee.

Public Company Audit Oversight Board

http://pcaobus.org

The Public Company Audit Oversight Board (PCAOB) is a nonprofit corporation established by Congress to oversee the audits of public companies in order to protect the interests of investors and further the public interest in the preparation of informative, accurate, and independent audit reports. The PCAOB also oversees the audits of broker-dealers, including compliance reports filed pursuant to federal securities laws, to promote investor protection.

The Society of Corporate Secretaries & Governance Professionals
www.ascs.org

Originally founded as the American Society of Corporate Secretaries (ASCS), the Society of Corporate Secretaries & Governance Professionals (the society) acts as a positive force for enlightened corporate governance. The Society's key mission is to promote excellence in corporate governance. The Society's members address issues of public disclosure under the securities laws and matters affecting corporate governance, including the structure and meetings of boards of directors and their committees, as well as the proxy process and the annual meeting of shareholders and shareholder relations, particularly with large institutional owners.

U.S. Securities and Exchange Commission
www.sec.gov

The mission of the SEC is to protect investors, maintain fair, orderly, and efficient markets, and facilitate capital formation. The SEC issues and enforces rules that impact all public companies, particularly in regards to timely disclosure of meaningful financial and other information to the public.

Printed in the United States
By Bookmasters